HELL is for REAL

why it matters

HELL is or REAL

why it matters

GARY FRAZIER

First printing: February 2015

New Leaf Press, P.O. Box 726, Green Forest, AR 72638

New Leaf Press is a division of the New Leaf Publishing Group, Inc.

ISBN: 978-0-89221-732-8
Library of Congress Number: 2014957804

Cover by Diana Bogardus

Unless otherwise noted, all Scripture is from the King James Version (KJV) of the Bible.

Please consider requesting that a copy of this volume be purchased by your local library system.

Printed in the United States of America

Please visit our website for other great titles:
www.newleafpress.net

For information regarding author interviews,
please contact the publicity department at (870) 438-5288

New Leaf Press
A Division of New Leaf Publishing Group
www.newleafpress.net

Dedication

Writing this book has taken hours of prayer, research, application of knowledge gleaned over 40-plus years of Bible study, patience, and more prayer! However, I could not have completed this work without the constant encouragement of my gift from God — my precious wife who makes each day a little taste of heaven as we walk side by side along life's exciting journey heavenward.

Contents

The ultimate tragedy is that all those who end in Hell will have chosen it. Instead of accepting that we are all sinners in need of the salvation of Jesus Christ, their pride condemns them to spiritual death. In the end, someone must be god of our lives. If we insist on being our own god, we shall succeed, but at the cost of an eternity in Hell.

— GRANT R. JEFFREY
Heaven: The Mystery of Angels

foreword

There has always been and I suspect always will be a keen quiet interest in what happens to us when we die. Granted, most of the discussion surrounding one's certain demise is relegated to a conversation upon the deathbed should one be fortunate enough to have that kind of earthly exit. For others, the conversation never takes place due to an unforeseen, sudden accident claiming their earthly lives. Rarely is there ever an open and honest talk about the reality of one's own mortality. Death seems to be a taboo topic, yet it is a certainty. Nonetheless, in these days of political upheaval on almost every continent coupled with a sense of hopelessness and loss of direction worldwide, there seems to be a renewed interest in the afterlife. Television programs, movies, and books abound with thoughts concerning the afterlife. Hollywood is in sync with this current trend and is seeking to give the public what the public wants — information and entertainment concerning the afterlife. Television presents us with titles such as *Forever* (with the subtitle *What could you do with eternity?*), *The Afterlife, Sea of Souls, Being Human, The Fades,* and many more.

While the media are hyping their philosophy concerning the future, others are looking into biblical prophecies and teachings surrounding the end times. The theme is prevalent in books, both Christian and secular, as well as in popular movies. To read or watch some of these works is to receive a potpourri of intrigue, mystery, make-believe, and the latest in special effects, with only a smattering of biblical truth.

It is in this climate that I welcome my good friend Gary Frazier's book, *Hell Is for Real*. Gary leads us on a quest for truth — truth about our future! Can we really know what our future holds? Does anyone have answers? Do all people go to heaven when they die? What really happens to us when we die? Using the story of a typical American family as a backdrop, Gary walks us through the sequence of events that is in the future for each of us. Through the eyes and experiences of the imaginary Rhodes family, we see the reality of death, eternity spent in heaven or in hell, the Rapture of the Church, the Judgment Seat of Christ or the *Bema*, the Marriage Supper, the Tribulation, the Second Coming, Armageddon, the millennial reign of Christ, and the Great White Throne Judgment. For some of you these are familiar terms, while for others I'm speaking a foreign language! These are all specific events and times that indeed will occur in the future. Only God knows when these events will take place. The specific dates will unfold according to His divine timetable. Gary explains this timetable in detail, defining the terminology and presenting the various theories or schools of thought surrounding the last days, as he is uniquely qualified to do so.

In recent years, Gary Frazier has virtually lived in the Holy Land, teaching, preaching, studying, and observing — first hand — the current issues and happenings in the Middle East and how they relate to the biblical prophecies surrounding that land. He has a great love and passion for Israel and its people as well as an unquenchable interest in events past, present, and future surrounding its history. Because of this, I believe he has tremendous credibility as a teacher of future events.

Although *Hell Is for Real* is a theological study, it is illustrative and practical so that you do not have to be a theologian to understand it. Not only will you benefit from Gary's insight and instruction, but you will also experience his passion and sense of urgency for men and women to know God's plan for their lives and to receive His sacrificial offering of His only begotten Son.

Death — it's real, it's final, and as in the case of the Rhodes family, it will happen to you and to me one day. Hebrews 9:27 states, *"It is appointed unto men once to die, but after this the judgment."* We all have a reservation — one we will keep whether we want to or not. Heaven or hell!

So continue reading! When you do, you will discover gold in these pages as you are compelled to examine your own heart and life and are drawn to Jesus Christ — the One who will come again to rule and reign throughout eternity and before whom every knee will bow and every tongue will confess as "King of kings and Lord of lords."

— Ed Young, Senior Pastor
Second Baptist Church, Houston, Texas

For what shall it profit a man, if he shall gain the whole world, and lose his own soul?

— JESUS CHRIST
Mark 8:36

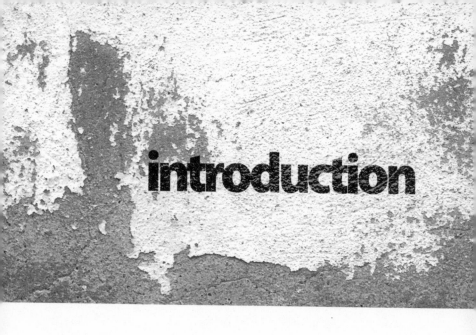

introduction

He's the cutest little boy I have ever seen in person or on screen! I'm referring to Connor Corum, who plays Colton Burpo in the recent movie *Heaven Is for Real*. When this little fellow looks up and smiles, the whole world lights up. I have no idea where they found him. Most likely, he's been acting since he was a toddler, but he is a find indeed and he simply melts your heart. Recently my wife, Sandra, and I watched this heartwarming, interesting movie, not seeking to discover if heaven is for real or not, since the Bible already tells us, but rather to see why so many of our friends found it — that is, the movie and the book — so compelling.

I had read the book not long after it first came out in 2011, simply because there was such a buzz about it among so many of the churches in which I was speaking. I was constantly being asked if I had read the book, and if so, what did I think about it? "Is it for real?" was the question I was asked over and over again. In order to be able to respond truthfully, I read *Heaven Is for Real* not once but twice. Through the years, I've read many books and articles about people who supposedly die and go to either heaven or hell; frankly, I've dismissed most of them as fantasy, preferring instead to go to the Word of God with any questions I have had concerning the afterlife.

As we watched the movie, I began to get a very strong sense that while it was never stated, there was an underlying, subliminal message that I had not noticed while reading the book. That message, simply put, was that in the end, everyone goes to heaven! Everyone. Is this true? Do all people, no matter what they have said, done, or become in their days on earth, really end up in heaven? Where does this idea come from? Is this what the Bible teaches? Is this what God's Word says? Is this what Jesus taught? Is this what the Apostles understood? Is this what the New Testament Church preached and believed? And if this is true, then how do we get there — instantly, or is there some path we walk? Some philosophy we accept? Some creed to which we ascribe? Some prescribed circuitous route we take to get there? Do we really meet St. Peter at the gates of heaven and get asked to spell hippopotamus? Once we are there, do we remain a child, a teen, or adult? Are we locked into the same age as when we died? Are babies who die still babies? Do we, in fact, see all our relatives who have died before us, including those whom we never met on earth? Does Jesus take us by the hand and lead us around heaven on a grand sightseeing tour of time? Is it possible for one to return to earth and resume a normal life after such an experience?

Please understand that I am not attacking little Colton Burpo and the experience he claims to have had, and neither am I criticizing his parents, who told his story and their experiences. However, as a Christ follower, minister, and teacher of the Word of God for more than 40 years, I must say that while I loved the movie and the book before it, the movie is essentially just a Hollywood production. It's an entertaining way to spend approximately 99 minutes. The real issue at stake, however, is one that we must not view merely as entertainment or fantasy.

Why? Because death and eternity — not a movie — is our reality! Death is a coming attraction, and it's coming to your life! Death is a 100 percent certainty for every single human being who walks this planet. Each of us has a reservation, a divine appointment. Every kid in your class will die at some point! Every person in the office, the warehouse, the restaurant, the factory, or doctor's office where you work will die! Every neighbor on your street or in your building will end up in a grave! Every famous and infamous person will depart this life one day! This is not Hollywood. This is reality. Just look at the obituary page in your newspaper or on the web as proof of this. Every class reunion I attend, there are fewer and fewer of my classmates in attendance. In light of this stark and glaringly ominous truth, what am I, what are you, what are we to do?

Let me suggest that we begin with a search for truth. We must seek to find if there is a reliable source — one in which we can trust. Are the words of this four-year-old boy to be trusted? Was this precious child given the answers sought after by generations of people who have inhabited planet Earth? I'll let you make that decision for yourself at the end of our quest, but I urge you to first carefully ponder the facts I'll present. I urge you to choose wisely in light of what we will discover. This is not a decision you should make because the little boy is such a darling. Why? Simply put — what if the little boy is wrong? Your assessment should not be based on emotion. Why? Because emotions are feelings and you can't trust feelings.

What if everyone doesn't go to heaven in the end? What if even the majority of people don't go to heaven in the end? What about the people who claim to have died and gone to hell and yet returned? Are we to accept their story as well because their experience is vastly different from Colton Burpo's?

We will explore the answers to these questions in the remaining pages of this book. Together we will search for the truth, and should we discover it, I will encourage each of us to act upon it. However, I do want you to know I have already done the search for us. I have discovered the truth that heaven is for real, but so is hell! How do we know this? The Bible! The Bible does not leave us ignorant of those things that are ahead. While it does not give every detail about the future and the life beyond, the Bible most definitely does give us all the "need to know" information to prepare for an eternal existence. It really comes down to whether or not you accept the authority of the Bible as God's Word or you choose to ignore it and take man's word concerning eternity. What if the Bible is right and man is wrong? Are you willing to take that gamble since the stakes are so high?

In the chapters ahead, we will explore the destiny of those who know the Lord Jesus Christ as their personal Savior and those who have rejected Him as Lord of life. We will follow a time line, a chronology of coming attractions, if you please, of the events to come. Along that timeline, we will discover what will happen to both the believer — the one who chooses to accept Jesus Christ as Lord, the Bible and the truths contained within it, as well as the unbeliever — the one who chooses to ignore the Lord Jesus and biblical truth. The two will face starkly contrasting destinies.

In this context, you will be introduced to two generations of the fictional Rhodes family of Normal, Ohio. Harold Rhodes died in 1999 and went immediately to hell. His wife, Betty, followed him in death four years later. She loved the Lord Jesus Christ, and as a dedicated follower immediately went to be with her Lord Jesus in heaven. You will follow the destinies of these two senior Rhodes. Then you will meet Harold and Betty's son, Henry, who is left behind at the Rapture of the Church when Jesus makes good on His promise to come collect His followers. Henry will live through the unprecedented trials of the Tribulation that come upon the world in the most horrific seven years the world has experienced or ever will. At the same time, you will follow the destiny of Henry's wife, Helen, a devout believer who experiences the Rapture, the Judgment Seat of Christ, the Marriage Supper of the Lamb, the Second Coming of Jesus, the thousand-year reign of Christ, and the eternal order. Please do not let these terms bewilder you, as each of them will be completely defined and clearly explained.

The next event on God's timetable will be the Rapture, or the coming of Christ for the saints, the saved. It is true that the English word *rapture* does not appear in the biblical text itself. The word derives from the Latin *raptere,* which means "to snatch away or to catch away." Regardless, *rapture* is an excellent word to capture the meaning of St. Paul's description of the great scene in which living believers will be *caught up* to be with the Lord (1 Thessalonians 4:17). But those alive at that climactic moment will not precede those believers who have died prior to this event. Those believers shall be raised; that is, here will be a physical resurrection of the body from the dead — infused with the spirit that never dies — and the resurrected believers will lead the vanguard into the heavens above. Those living believers will be changed in the twinkling of an eye, with their glorified bodies following immediately behind them.

On the other hand, those who are not believers will be left behind, continuing with their day-to-day lives. The Lord Jesus makes this clear in His most extensive teaching concerning this often-queried subject. He indicates this stark truth in the words, "Then two men will be in the field: one will be taken and the other left. Two women will be grinding at the mill: one will be taken and the other left" (Matthew 24:40–41; NKJV). The world as we know it will not end with the Rapture of the believers. There will be a great population left behind on planet Earth. The Church will be gone and the Holy Spirit will be gone in the sense that the Spirit dwelling in the believer, and the presence of

Christ amidst His people will cease to exist. The world will get exactly what it always wanted — the total absence of Jesus Christ and His people.

Thus, after the Rapture, there will begin a seven-year period that Jeremiah the prophet referred to as *the time of Jacob's trouble* (Jeremiah 30:7). Jesus described it by saying, "For then shall be great tribulation, such as was not since the beginning of the world to this time, no, nor ever shall be" (Matthew 24:21). This unprecedented period will last for seven years according to Daniel 9:24–27. Revelation 6:1–17 describes in detail the unleashing of horrible, unspeakable, unimaginable wrath on the God-forsaken planet. The world that rejected Christ will have the opportunity to live in a world without Him. Never could the imagination of depraved humanity conceive what will happen during that time.

In the very midst of this period will be the desecration of the rebuilt temple in Jerusalem (Matthew 24:15). The abomination of desolation will transpire (Daniel 9:27; 2 Thessalonians 2:2–4). And the lost on earth will experience the full blast of these events.

But what will the saved in heaven be doing? These seven years shall be a time of evaluation of the saints based on the *quality of* their doctrine and life and service (1 Corinthians 3:11–17). This is the judgment of the *Bema* or the Judgment Seat of Christ. This will not be judgment for salvation or damnation. Rather it will be a judgment of the quality of Christian life, service, and doctrine. The result of the scrutiny will be the granting or the loss of rewards to believers based on that quality. While all hell, in a literal sense, is breaking loose in the Tribulation on earth below, the transported Christian will receive the appropriate reward in heaven.

At the end of that period will be the Second Coming of Christ, the coming of Christ with the saints (Matthew 24:29–

31; Revelation 19:11–21). This will not be the sudden, silent, selective removal of the Church. This will be the glorious, visible return of the risen and reigning Christ. This will be the warrior judge coming to claim what rightly belongs to Him. After the Battle of Armageddon, the victorious Christ will reign on earth for one thousand years (Revelation 20:1–6). The unbelievers who are alive at the return of Christ will be immediately sent to hell to await their final judgment (Matthew 25:41–46). The Tribulation saints, those who come to faith in Christ (Yeshua) during the Tribulation and are martyred, will immediately be transformed and join the returning army of saints in their glorified bodies. The innumerable multitude who come to faith during the Tribulation and manage to survive will join the host of the ages, enter the millennium in their physical bodies, and continue to procreate. At the end of the thousand-year reign of Christ on the earth, there will be the final judgment of the unbelieving and spiritually lost. This will be a day of unimaginable despair in which the doomed and damned will be given their final sentence — endless torment in hell, forever separated from God and their loved ones. In the eternal state, the saved will spend eternity with God in heaven and the lost will spend eternity with Satan and his demons in the fire of hell. What a division of humanity this shall be!

Matthew 24:1–14

Then Jesus went out and departed from the temple, and His disciples came up to show Him the buildings of the temple. ²And Jesus said to them, "Do you not see all these things? Assuredly, I say to you, not one stone shall be left here upon another, that shall not be thrown down."

³Now as He sat on the Mount of Olives, the disciples came to Him privately, saying, "Tell us, when will

these things be? And what will be the sign of Your coming, and of the end of the age?"

[4]And Jesus answered and said to them: "Take heed that no one deceives you. [5]For many will come in My name, saying, 'I am the Christ,' and will deceive many. [6]And you will hear of wars and rumors of wars. See that you are not troubled; for all these things must come to pass, but the end is not yet. [7]For nation will rise against nation, and kingdom against kingdom. And there will be famines, pestilences, and earthquakes in various places. [8]All these are the beginning of sorrows.

[9]"Then they will deliver you up to tribulation and kill you, and you will be hated by all nations for My name's sake. [10]And then many will be offended, will betray one another, and will hate one another. [11]Then many false prophets will rise up and deceive many. [12]And because lawlessness will abound, the love of many will grow cold. [13]But he who endures to the end shall be saved. [14]And this gospel of the kingdom will be preached in all the world as a witness to all the nations, and then the end will come" (NKJV).

What is hell? Hell is oneself.
Hell is alone, the other figures in it
Merely projections.
There is nothing to escape from
And nothing to escape to.
One is always alone.

— T.S. ELIOT
The Cocktail Party

1
the reality of mortality

As Queen Elizabeth lay dying, surrounded by the splendor of her palace, she reportedly uttered the famous words, "My kingdom for an inch of time." The most powerful woman in the world could not stop the falling shadow of death. George Burns was already booked to perform in Las Vegas on his 100th birthday, but he could not stop an earlier appointment with mortality. Young and handsome John F. Kennedy Jr. and his beautiful wife had the same date. Revered football legend Tom Landry, who seemed immortal, could not stop the moment. The day he died, the beloved cartoonist of Peanuts fame, Charles Schultz, also died. None could stop the reality of mortality. Each and every January, the list is published to remind us of the deaths of the famous and infamous who died in the previous 12 months. While normally rather lengthy, the list, published by *Us Weekly* magazine, usually includes only those with recognizable names. The year 2013 saw the deaths of celebrities such as actors Cory Monteith and James Gandolfini, film critic Roger Ebert, and swimmer Ester Williams, to name a few. The year 2014 has already seen the likes of actors Philip Seymour Hoffman, Shirley

Temple, Robin Williams, Lauren Bacall, former Reagan White House Press Secretary James Brady, and others. Here's the point: we all die!

Our youth-and-fitness-obsessed culture remains intoxicated with the allure of life that will not end. Even though there are more centenarians alive today than ever before, they too face mortality.

We are temporary. We are transient. Every grave marker in every cemetery on this planet is a witness to that reality. Go to the cemetery. Look at a granite marker. Visualize the inescapable fact that someday your name will be on a stone just like that, with a date of birth and a date of death. Unless you happen to live in the generation that witnesses the Rapture of the Church, you will leave this planet by the same route as everyone else (with the exception of Enoch and Elijah). Enoch walked with God and was raptured away into heaven without ever having faced physical death (Genesis 5:24). Elijah was caught up in a fiery chariot and likewise skipped death (2 Kings 2:11). I have never known anyone who has had these kinds of experiences, have you?

Thanks to Leonardo DiCaprio and Kate Winslet, the end of the 20th century witnessed a fatal attraction to a famous shipwreck that occurred at the beginning of the century — the sinking of the *Titanic*. The world riveted its attention on the loss of a ship with more than 1,500 fatalities in the early morning hours of April 15, 1912, in the icy waters of the Atlantic. One young person wearing a T-shirt at O'Hare airport in Chicago captured the truth of the matter. The T-shirt read, "The ship sank; get over it." In fact, we are all on the *Titanic*. It is called planet Earth. Nobody journeys forever.

One of the earliest to write on this subject, Viktor Frankl, an Austrian-born neurologist and psychiatrist as well as Holocaust survivor, mused that no man can really contemplate his own death. That may indeed be the case, but is it that man cannot or that man will not? Man's ultimate destiny is to die. Arnold Toynbee, the philosopher and historian, put it this way:

> Man alone . . . has foreknowledge of his coming death . . . and, possessing this foreknowledge, has a chance, if he chooses to take it, of pondering over the strangeness of his destiny. . . . He has at least a possibility of coping with it, since he is endowed with the capacity to think about it in advance and . . . to face it and to deal with it in some way that is worthy of human dignity.[1]

Daily we are reminded in numerous ways of the often sudden and unexpected reality of death as we view wars, acts of terrorism, and violence in our cities, our nations, and our world. We know it is real, we know it exists, yet we just cannot seem to come to terms with it. In our Internet, cell phone, fax machine, voice mail, overnight delivery, fast-track society, death seems to be an unpleasant interruption of the action. Yet no new technology has changed the old reality. Everybody dies. Each of us has a date with death. Some place their hope in cloning to preserve them forever. Others believe in cryogenics and have their mortal remains frozen until the day a cure will be found for their cause of death. Some actually believe that brains will be transplanted in the skulls of volunteers who will take on the old brain of a very rich person.

John D. Rockefeller Sr. built the greatest fortune in American history until that of Bill Gates, whose wealth has now been surpassed by that of Mark Zuckerberg of *Facebook* fame. Rockefeller was the founder and power behind Standard Oil. He and his son spent a large portion of their lives trying to give away all of the money Rockefeller Sr. had made. As the richest man on the planet, Rockefeller had a single obsession: he wanted to

---

1. Arnold Toynbee, "Traditional Attitudes Towards Death," in *Man's Concern With Death*, ed. Arnold Toynbee et al. (New York: McGraw, 1968), p. 63.

stay alive. As such, he founded hospitals and advanced research centers for the study of longevity. He meticulously studied the latest research on long life. He wanted to live to be a hundred, but he died just short of that mark. The richest man in the world, with all the resources to stave off the inevitable, could not stop it.

Every biography ends with an obituary. The pianist plays his last note. The carpenter hammers his final nail. The barber cuts his final head of hair. The homemaker washes her last dish. The athlete runs his final mile. The teacher utters her final lesson. Yet this generation, in a way unlike any other, lives with a blissful refusal to acknowledge this absolute reality: we are mortal.

I write these words to inform you of your mortality. You will die. But that will not be the end of you. Plants die and decompose. Animals die and their lives are gone forever. Human beings die and face another dimension of eternal existence. Ever since God breathed into Adam's nostrils the breath of life, every human who ever drew a breath on this planet lasts forever. Abraham and Sarah, Isaac and Rebekah, Hitler and Eva Braun, Elvis and John Lennon, and the entire roll call of humanity, both famous and obscure, will have a conscious existence forever.

So will you.

This book presents to you the two destinations that define the eternal existence of every individual who ever died. One destination holds inescapable horror and eternal retribution. The other is one of release, reward, rest, and reunion. There could not be a greater contrast between the two.

Harold Rhodes died and went to hell. His wife, Betty, died and went to heaven. Their son, Henry, an unbeliever like his father, lived through the Rapture and survived the Tribulation. Jesus then returned to earth to separate the saved from the unsaved. But when Henry stood before the Great White Throne Judgment, he (like his reprobate father) was sentenced to an eternity in hell. Meanwhile, in heaven, Betty gathered around the throne of God with her daughter-in-law Helen.

This is not fiction. You will spend eternity either in heaven or in hell. You may make fun of this now, ridicule it, and try to forget it. But I can guarantee you one thing: you will think about it when you double over with a heart attack, your vision dims, and your breath goes away. If the doctor tells you that you have cancer and three months to live, you will think about this. If you have a peaceful deathbed and your family gathers around to watch you die, you will think of this. I would rather you consider me harsh now and thank God in eternity that you listened to me than to like me now and burn in hell forever. It is that straightforward.

You would do well to take this seriously. I have visited with businessmen on their deathbeds. Eternity is breathing down their necks. Their hearts weaken. Their breathing becomes shallow. Their palms are perspiring. Guess what? Not one of them has ever said, "I wish I could spend one more day at the office." None of them has ever pled for time to make one more deal. They are suddenly aware that they are about to step into eternity.

You should read this book with the same intensity with which you would read it if your physician just told you that you had six months to live. It can forever change your destiny and that of those around you.

There are only two kinds of people in the end: those who say to God, "Thy will be done," and those to whom God says, in the end, "Thy will be done." All that are in Hell, choose it. Without that self-choice there could be no Hell. No soul that seriously and constantly desires joy will ever miss it. Those who seek find. Those who knock it is opened.

— C.S. LEWIS
The Great Divorce

2
fake funerals and perjured preachers

"We have gathered together here today to honor the memory of Harold Rhodes. His wife, Betty, son, Henry, and daughter-in-law, Helen, survive him. I want you to know Harold died and went to hell."

How many times have you heard a funeral begin with those words? I can venture a guess — never! I have never said those words nor have you heard those words at any funeral, anywhere. In fact, I have never heard the word *hell* spoken at any funeral. If we talk about hell at all, we do so generally, theoretically, and theologically. But when it comes to identifying a given person who died and went there, we balk. We just can't seem to bring ourselves to be that honest at a funeral. *On Death and Dying*, written by Elisabeth Kubler-Ross in 1969, which has long been the model for that subject in the world of psychiatry, reminds me of the numerous conversations I have overheard at funerals through the years. Most conversations find attendees talking about sports, weather, travel, or current events. Rarely, and I mean rarely, have I heard someone honestly speak about dying, the death of the individual, and what will happen to them. In her work, Kubler-Ross describes five psychological stages of dying, and denial is the first.[2] We just cannot, nor are we willing to, speak honestly about the eternal destination of a named person.

In that regard, I need to ask your forgiveness. In fact, all of us in the ministry need to ask your forgiveness. I lied. We all lied. Please do not judge us too harshly or too quickly. There is a reason we fake it at funerals and perjure ourselves as preachers. We want to comfort people. It is a professional expectation. We believe what Paul wrote when he prayed, ". . . that we may be able to comfort those who are in any trouble, with the comfort with which we ourselves are comforted by God" (2 Corinthians 1:4; NKJV). We want to bring consolation to grieving people. But in reality, we have lied. Recently, while driving from Naples, Florida, north to Tampa on I-75, a billboard caught my eye. It read: "Live your life in such a way that the preacher doesn't have to lie at your funeral!" Isn't this what really happens over and over again?

Consider this. A man who in his lifetime never showed any interest in God or the things of God is lying in a casket. He loved his business, his golf game, his country club, his lake house, and his cars. So we preach at the funeral that he was a great businessman. We remember how much he enjoyed golf. We recognize his membership in the Rotary or country club, but at the same time, we totally avoid the obvious. This man had no interest whatsoever in anything remotely related to God, Christ, the gospel, or even the Church. We picture him sitting and singing praises to God forever, when he could not stand to be in church one hour a week praising God. We conclude that he is with the holy Apostles and the saints of the ages forever, when he would rather have been in the card room at the club

---

2. Elisabeth Kubler-Ross, *On Death and Dying* (New York, NY: Scribner, 1969).

smoking cigars, drinking gin, and playing poker. Before you think I am exaggerating, just remember some of the funerals you have attended.

At one funeral, the preacher waxed on and on with soaring eloquence about the deceased's devotion to his family, his church, and his God. After about 30 minutes of this, his widow whispered to one of the sons, "Go lift the lid of that casket and see if that is your father in there. I think we are in the wrong place." While this may seem humorous in one sense, no doubt some families certainly must have felt that way at memorial services many times.

We find shallow solace in the flimsy memory that 35 years earlier, a man walked down the aisle in a church, filled out a card, was immersed in water or sprinkled, and then, for the rest of his life, never gave any evidence whatsoever that Christ had changed his life. We preach him into a heaven where redeemed saints will spend eternity singing the praises of a Jesus who was a total stranger to the man.

Such preaching reminds me of the story of an ineffective surgeon. The surgeon was famous for conducting many operations. When patients were wheeled into the operating room, the surgeon and his assistants were immaculately robed in the finest scrubs. The operating room itself was state-of-the-art. The hospital was famous, as was the surgeon. After the patient was anesthetized, the surgeon would make a few futile passes over the patient's skin with a sharp scalpel. Yet a strange thing happened. When the patients were wheeled out of the operating room to the ICU, they never got better. In fact, they died. The surgeon remained famous. He kept on operating. Patients kept on dying. Nothing was ever said.

Finally, a first-year intern, a rather dull and plodding student, dared to state the obvious. No incision was ever made. The scalpel never cut the skin. The whole procedure in the operating room was a mere charade. The surgeon — a highly trained man in a beautiful gown, wielding a sharp knife — never really cut the patient open. Patient after patient never got any better.

Is this not exactly what happens in most churches Sunday after Sunday? Highly trained ministers, some in beautiful doctoral robes, others in Armani suits, stand in famous institutions with the sword of the Spirit in their hands but never really use it to cut. They make a futile pass over the congregation with some platitudes about how to win over worry or how to manage finances, but they never state the obvious. Many preachers today are so concerned about political correctness that they simply refuse to preach the whole truth of God's Word. In fact, in many churches, Jesus has been presented in a way that simply cannot be found in the Scriptures. Yes, God is love but He is also pure, holy, and just and will not, nor can He, tolerate sin. This shallow, sickly, and anemic portrait of Jesus is just wrong.

The result of this kind of man-centered preaching is in sharp contrast to the outcome on the Day of Pentecost when Peter preached that the resurrected Jesus was God in the flesh whom they had crucified. On that day, the hearers were cut to the heart, convicted of their sin and need for redemption. But not today! Week after week, Sunday after Sunday, people go to church and are never warned. They are never upset. They are never challenged with eternity. In other words, they are never cut! They leave church in the same condition in which they arrived, go to the restaurant, go home, and fall asleep watching a ball game, never convicted of their sin and need for redemption by the Word of God. They are never warned that they are going to hell without a relationship with God through Jesus Christ. This deviation from truth was clearly exhibited to the world by a letter from Dr. Robert Schuller, a disciple of the late Norman Vincent Peale, published in the October 5, 1984, issue of *Christianity Today* in which he stated,

I don't think anything has been done in the name of Christ and under the banner of Christianity that has proven more destructive to human personality and, hence, counterproductive to the evangelical enterprise than the often crude, uncouth, and unchristian strategy of attempting to make people aware of their lost and sinful condition.[3]

Why is it that in the vast majority of churches in America the only time people ever hear about eternity is during a funeral service? Why do they never hear about hell at the 11 o'clock hour on Sunday morning? Why have the "men of God" become so afraid of *them* — that is, the people in the pew — that they disobey *Him*?

The first reason is *entertainment*. The entertainment industry in its various forms has done its best to present a convenient *universalism*. In the Hollywood version of eternity, everybody goes to heaven. Shows such as *Touched by an Angel, If I Stay, Heaven Can Wait, Always, Ghost, Forever: What Could You Do For Eternity, The Ghost Whisperer*, and many others send everybody to heaven. And what a heaven it is! Even Burt Reynolds played God in one film. Never in the Hollywood version of eternity does anyone ever die and go to hell. You may find it strange coming from a minister, but I understand Hollywood's stated motive — that is, to provide entertainment. Who wants to pay money to see a movie that upsets them? How many would pony up from 5 to 15 dollars for a movie ticket, only to be confronted with their own sin nature and the consequences it does and will bring? Never forget, it's all about the money! I understand.

However, yet another motive in Hollywood today is clearly expressed in its productions. The motive is both religious and political, and they are tightly wound together. Some have said that

3. Robert Schuller, "Dr. Schuller Comments" (letter to the editor), *Christianity Today* (October 5, 1984), 12–13.

when Satan was thrown out of heaven he landed in *Holywood* (no it is not misspelled; there was a time when they turned out wholesome movies void of attacks on the family, void of filthy language, void of sex, and without a hint of perversion) and changed it to Hollywood.

A second reason is *education*. There is no doubt that a full-scale war exists in the realm of education. The war is one in which the victor claims the minds of the young, who then influence the next generation with their views. In other words, the student becomes the teacher and so on. That war began in a courtroom in 1925 in the small, economically depressed town of Dayton, Tennessee. The trial concerned whether children would continue to be taught that God created the world and all that is therein, including every human being, or would be taught that man was a product of chance as propagated by Charles Darwin's *Theory of Evolution*. However, the fact is that the entire case boiled down to whether or not we as a people, as a nation, accept God's Word as truth over man's word. The verdict became clear, and man's word triumphed. Theistic evolution won the day (see Notes for a complete explanation). The change that began that miserably hot summer day in Tennessee has and is continuing to change the worldview of generations. That decision ultimately led to another watershed moment in 1963 when prayer, Bible reading, and God were banned from public schools in America. The days when I sat at my desk in the classroom and heard a reading from the Word of God, followed by a prayer led by a student, had come to an end, and America was on her way to moral depravity.

In addition, there are much broader cultural reasons for the absence of anything like a straightforward and honest word about hell. Hell is an embarrassment in the Church today because of several factors. Allow me to consider just two of them.

Cultural Pluralism

Christians in general, and the sub group defined as evangelical Christians in particular, are far more educated and well-traveled than ever before. We have been to college. We have taken trips to Europe and the Far East. We have seen secularism in England, once a great lighthouse for the gospel. We have been exposed to Islam in the Middle East, Buddhism in Japan, and Hinduism in India. We are overwhelmed with the religious diversity in the world around us. We are broad-minded. We are eclectic in our thinking. We are religiously tolerant. We gradually forget the sharp distinction between the teachings of Jesus Christ and the platitudes of other world religions. We lower the bar. We relax our thinking. We do not want to deal with the exclusive and absolute truth claims of Jesus Christ, who demanded total allegiance to Him as the only road to heaven. We forget His statement: *"I am the way, the truth, and the life. No one comes to the Father, except through me"* (John 14:6; NKJV).

We must see clearly that the problem is not that there is not some good to be found in all religions but that Jesus makes no allowance for any other path to God. Oprah Winfrey's statement to her following of 22 million makes it very clear what she believes: "One of the mistakes that human beings make is believing that there is only one way to live." She went on to say, "Instead, there are many paths to what you call God."[4]

Perhaps U2's lead singer Bono shed some interesting light on this serious subject when he took a stand for Jesus and who He is. When asked if he thought it was far-fetched for Jesus to be the Son of God, he replied, "No, it's not far-fetched to me. Look, the secular response to the Christ story always goes like this: He was a great prophet, obviously a very interesting guy,

---

4. http://www.renewamerica.com/columns/mwest/120507, http://www.jesus-is-savior.com/Wolves/oprah-fool.htm.

had a lot to say along the lines of other great prophets, be they Elijah, Muhammad, Buddha, or Confucius. But actually Christ doesn't allow you that. He doesn't let you off the hook. Christ says, 'No, I'm not saying I'm a teacher, don't call me a teacher. I'm not saying I'm a prophet . . . I'm saying **I'm God incarnate**.' "[5] Wow! That's about as blunt and truthful as it gets. I really don't think I've ever heard Bono say anything I agree with except this.

Today we are surrounded by many people who claim to be Christians and yet have bought wholeheartedly into the subtle, yet dangerous lies of the enemy, forgetting that truth is truth whether we believe it or not. We forget that truth is truth in every realm. Just because a Buddhist does not believe two plus two equals four does not change that truth. Just because a Moslem refuses to believe in gravity does not cause gravity to lose its force. We would consider that kind of thinking foolish and illogical. However, tolerance versus absolutes has pressed us into accepting various forms of Eastern religions as truth.

One of the world's truly outstanding Christian apologists is Ravi Zacharias. Born in Madras, India, and an atheist until he was 17, he grew up in a moderate Anglican home. Zacharias has taught and spoken all over the world regarding the validity of Christianity as opposed to world religions. In speaking about Jesus and the supposed *many paths to God* he states, "In all of these [World Religions] there emerges an instruction, a way of living. It is not Zoroaster to whom you turn. It is Zoroaster to whom you *listen*. It is not Buddha who delivers you; it is his Noble Truths that instruct you. It is not Mohammad who transforms you; it is the beauty of the Koran that woos you. By contrast, Jesus did not only teach or expound His message. *He was identical to His message.*"[6]

---

5. http://www.patheos.com/blogs/frankviola/bono-on-jesus/.

6. Ravi Zacharias, *Jesus Among Other Gods* (Nashville, TN: Thomas Nelson, Inc., 2009), p. 89, emphasis in original.

We should remember that the truth about heaven and hell is not a relative truth. Some of us think that hell *used to be* the truth but no longer is the truth. We consider hell to be a recollection of Dante's *Inferno* that scared the serfs into submission in the High Middle Ages but not a reality for an Internet world. It just does not fit into our relativistic view of modern culture.

Theological Liberalism

Beginning with the Enlightenment and continuing into the 21st century, the Church has been assaulted by theological liberalism. In its broadest definition, such liberalism sits in judgment of the Word of God. It determines what is inspired and what is not. It's what I call a Dalmatian theology. It declares that the Bible is inspired in spots, and the liberal theologian is inspired to pick the spots.

One of liberalism's high priests was Rudolph Bultmann, the German theologian who taught at the University of Marburg. Bultmann concluded that modern humans were unwilling to accept the Bible's version of a miraculous universe. Thus, Bultmann "de-mythologized" the Bible. He wanted to keep the ethical core of Jesus' teachings while ridding that kernel of its miraculous husk. One of the first things to disappear in his program was the very notion of an eternal hell. Such pagan thought had to be eradicated from the Bible. This eradication has taken two primary forms in the liberal theological world.

One form of theological liberalism is universalism. The theory of universalism declares that every person will go to heaven. It makes no difference what that person believed or how that person lived. The child rapist who is executed will go to heaven just as quickly as the missionary who died serving Jesus on a foreign field. Universalism is a mushy, comfortable, vague, hazy hope that everybody will go to heaven forever. The oft-spoken phrase, "We are all God's children," epitomizes this false concept.

Perhaps the best-known teacher of this heresy presently is Rob Bell. Although Bell says he believes some people will go to hell, he pictures hell as a purifying place where people will receive a second chance. In the preface of his book *Love Wins*, he writes, "A staggering number of people have been taught that a select few Christians will spend forever in a peaceful, joyous place called heaven, while the rest of humanity spends forever in torment and punishment in hell with no chance of anything better. . . . This is misguided and toxic and ultimately subverts the contagious spread of Jesus' message of love, peace, forgiveness, and joy."[7]

One of the most dangerous elements of this philosophy is that it begins with small questions and then progresses to an all-out open defiance of biblical authority. Demi Lovato is just one of many celebrities claiming to be a Christian. Recently she declared, "The LOVING God that I believe in would never condemn anyone for loving another human of the same sex."[8] So where does this refusal to accept biblical authority go next? The gate opens and out comes lesbian Christian rock star and supposed theologian (studied theology at Oxford) Vicky Beeching, who declared on August 15, 2014, "I feel certain God loves me just the way I am."[9]

Clearly, that loving God that I believe in, as they say, will never condemn anyone to hell! The issue is not about same-sex marriage or lesbianism, nor is it about hell. It is about TRUTH! Once Christians and church leaders cast aside the Word of God as the final authority of faith and practice, they move very quickly to the acceptance of theological liberalism and embrace abortion,

7. Rob Bell, *Love Wins: A Book About Heaven, Hell, and the Fate of Every Person Who Ever Lived* (New York: HarperOne, 2011).

8. http://www.motherjones.com/mixed-media/2014/07/demi-lovato-gay-rights-video-marriage-equality-human-rights-campaign.

9. http://www.christianpost.com/news/christian-rock-star-theologian-vicky-beeching-comes-out-as-lesbian-says-i-feel-certain-god-loves-me-just-the-way-i-am-124888/.

gay activism, and new age philosophy. For the most part they also become anti-Semitic, anti-Israel, and pro-Palestinian. While they still wear the label "Christian," they choose what they will accept or deny.

Thomas Jefferson, poster boy for the lie concerning the separation of Church and state, cut and pasted together his own Bible that suited his beliefs. Jefferson believed Jesus was a great moral teacher, but he could not accept the Resurrection of Jesus or the miracles he performed. The Jefferson Bible, or the *Life and Morals of Jesus of Nazareth* as it was called, was a cut and paste version of the New Testament. In other words, Jefferson wanted to pick and choose what suited him concerning the Word of God and the teachings of Jesus. He thus decided to simply ignore and dismiss whatever he deemed unimportant to him. Problem is, when he did that, in essence he was displacing God and placing himself upon the throne as God.

A more popular view has emerged among theological liberals and has even found currency among some evangelical scholars. That view is called "Annihilationism" or "conditional immortality." This view considers that every individual will be raised at the last day to appear before God. Every life will be reviewed, and only those who trusted in Christ or "lived for value" will enter into eternity. After judgment, those who did not pass the test will be obliterated, annihilated, and cease to live as conscious individuals. There will be for them a moment of judgment, a blast of fire, and then nothingness forever.

These two views are accommodating to the cultural pluralism and the theological relativism of the modern mind. They represent the modern world's attempt to rationalize the unpleasant reality of an eternal hell.

None of these views changes the nature of reality. I may stop believing the sun rises in the east, but that does not change the fact that it does. I may stand by Niagara Falls and deny that there is a roar of water, but that does not change the fact that there is. I may look over into the pit of hell and deny its reality, but that does not change the fact that it exists.

We're told that every 60 minutes, 287+ people go out into eternity. Just think — that is roughly 5 people every minute of every day! You will most definitely die if Jesus tarries. Hebrews 9:27 states the truth for all time: "And as it is appointed for men to die once, but after this the judgment" (NKJV). You have a date with deity, an appointment with the Almighty. Neither Hollywood nor the media will determine the nature of that date. Neither George Burns nor Burt Reynolds will be God. The Almighty God, maker of heaven and earth, will be God, and His Son Jesus will be your judge.

Modern American Christians simply refuse to consider, let alone believe, what the Bible says about hell. Jesus Christ said more about hell than did anyone else in the Bible. This book contains a simple message on a serious subject. Only a foolish person would die without the facts on eternal destiny. The only solid information we have on the subject of heaven and hell is the Word of God. The overwhelming majority of Americans, some 76 percent, believe in a heaven; 71 percent believe there is a hell, although their views on what that means vary greatly.[10] However, only one-half of 1 percent of them believe they are going there. This statistic in and of itself shows the great confusion about the nature of both heaven and hell.

Suppose with me for a moment that there was only a 10 percent chance that the Bible is correct in its clear teaching about an eternal hell. What if there was only a one in ten chance that it is right? If you were waiting at the airport to catch a plane and saw that one out of every ten planes taking off crashed and

---

10. "Americans Describe Their Views About Life After Death," Barna Group, October 21, 2003, https://www.barna.org/barna-update/article/5-barna-update/128-americans-describe-their-views-about-life-after-death#.VF0C3Yd-phi0.

> **Americans Describe Their Views About Life After Death:**
> Barna Group, October 21, 2003.
>
> 1,000 adults surveyed
> 76% believe in heaven
> 71% in hell
> Only ½ of 1% believe they are going to hell!

burned, what would you do? It might be the first, the fifth, or the ninth plane, but one out of every ten went down at the end of the runway in a great ball of fire. Would you fly? I doubt you would fly at all. If there was a 10 percent chance that your plane would not reach its destination, you would not dare get on that plane. You should approach this book with the same caution. If there is only a 10 percent chance that there is an eternal hell, should you not consider it seriously? Should you not seek the truth from God Himself?

Dateline: 1999

Betty Rhodes sat in the congregation at the funeral home while the minister gave the eulogy of Harold Rhodes. The liberal preacher intoned, "Harold Rhodes was a pillar of this community. He had perfect attendance at the Rotary for 30 years. He was a 20-year member at the Bent Shrub Country Club. You will notice by the presence of his lodge brothers on the front row that he was truly a man among men. . . ." Betty listened to this ministerial drivel, and, even in her grief, she regretted that the minister did not warn the congregation that those who died like her husband would go straight to hell.

She grieved for Harold with a grief that was beyond mere grief. As a godly woman who knew the eternal destiny of those who died with Christ and those who died without Him, she had the most reverent fear for the fate of her husband. She quietly prayed, through her tears, that the preacher would warn Harold's drinking buddies of the eternal fate of those who died without Christ. Yet the preacher droned on and on about Harold's life membership in the state university's alumni club, his total dedication to the motorcycle club and his trophy-winning stint on his bowling team. Poor Betty could not believe her ears.

"Harold never missed a charity chili cook-off," the minister continued, as if he had pronounced Harold worthy of the same honor as a missionary. Even Harold's lost friends wondered who in the world the preacher was talking about.

Harold was in no such state of amusement. The moment he doubled over with a heart attack while mowing his back yard, he sensed something more ominous than the heart attack. At first, Harold lay on the green grass, clawing it with his hands as if he could thereby hang onto his life. His self-propelled mower ran into the nearby fence and continued to whirl and gurgle in place. Harold felt the life going out of him. Indeed, in a moment he was looking down at his dead body on the ground. Harold wanted to go back. He wanted to finish the yard, go in, have a beer, and watch the sports show on ESPN as he always did. Instead, Harold was going away from everything he had ever known. Without saying a word, two enormous winged creatures carried Harold far away from his family, his mower, his yard, and Normal, Ohio.

More quickly than he could have imagined, Harold stood in a different world. He was in a place that was dark, hot, and lonely. The angelic beings pushed him through what looked like a door, and he fell through an abyss, a great gulf. Harold heard unearthly screams and felt a searing heat. A cackling demonic creature lunged at him and threw him into a fiery pit. Harold screamed, writhed, and begged somebody to help him. A leering demonic gargoyle spat on him and declared, "You will never get out of here. It will only get darker and hotter." Harold screamed again and tried to run out of the darkness. The farther he ran, the hotter and darker it became.

By the time the minister was bragging on old Harold, he had run so far into hell that he felt only darkness, heat, and distance from God, but most of all, isolation. Harold was completely alone. Where was the party he and his buddies used to joke about? How many times had Harold laughed and said, "Yeah, when I end up in hell we'll all have a big party." Harold found out he had been wrong all those times. No friends! No party! Harold was completely, totally alone!

Hell is not evil; it's a place where evil gets punished. Hell is not pleasant, appealing, or encouraging. But Hell is morally good, because a good God must punish evil.

— RANDY ALCORN
If God Is Good

3
hell: the suffering

There was a certain rich man, which was clothed in purple and fine linen, and fared sumptuously every day: and there was a certain beggar named Lazarus, which was laid at his gate, full of sores, and desiring to be fed with the crumbs which fell from the rich man's table: moreover the dogs came and licked his sores. And it came to pass, that the beggar died, and was carried by the angels into Abraham's bosom: the rich man also died, and was buried;

And in hell he lift up his eyes, being in torments, and seeth Abraham afar off, and Lazarus in his bosom. And he cried and said, Father Abraham, have mercy on me, and send Lazarus, that he may dip the tip of his finger in water, and cool my tongue; for I am tormented in this flame. But Abraham said, Son, remember that thou in thy lifetime receivedst thy good things, and likewise Lazarus evil things: but now he is comforted, and thou art tormented. And beside all this, between us and you there is a great gulf fixed: so that they which would pass from hence to you cannot; neither can they pass to us, that would come from thence. Then he said, I pray thee therefore, father, that thou wouldest send him to my father's house: for I have five brethren; that he may testify unto them, lest they also come into this place of torment. Abraham saith unto him, They have Moses and the prophets; let them hear them. And he said, Nay, father Abraham: but if one went unto them from the dead, they will repent. And he said unto him, If they hear not Moses and the prophets, neither will they be persuaded, though one rose from the dead (Luke 16:19–31).

Dateline Jerusalem

The scorching sun is beating down on the muscles and sinews of His exposed back that was shredded by the Roman whip. Lacerated, tormented by insects, bruised by beatings, and blinded by sweat, He carries a Roman cross through the streets of Jerusalem. The spittle and abuse from the crowd sting more than the swarming flies.

When He reaches His destination, the base of a barren, skull-like hill outside the city walls, He is told to lay down the instrument of His own execution. His hands are stretched out on the wood and nails are pounded through them. His feet are likewise pinned to the wood with iron nails. The Cross is lifted up high and dropped into a prepared hole in the rocky soil. The jolt rips through His body with a hellish pain. He hangs in the sun for six hours. His friends abandon Him. The crowd jeers at Him. Even the Supreme Court of the day scoffs at Him from beneath His Cross. Dehydrated, bleeding to death, blistered by the Judean sun, He dies. A sword is rammed into His body, breaking the pericardium around His heart. Water and blood flow out of His side. Jesus Christ is crucified. The Son of God is dead.

No more poignant picture of absolute suffering exists than the death of the Son of God by crucifixion. God sent His only begotten Son to the Cross for the salvation of humanity and of every human being who would believe and trust in Him. The world gave the infinite, perfect sacrifice of God its most degrading death. The world will go to hell for that.

Why will people experience the suffering of hell's torments? Will they feel the pain of hell because of lying? Lying is deceitful, injurious, and ruinous to careers and reputations. But people will not go to hell because they lied.

Will people go to hell because of adultery? There may be no greater pain in life than the pain of adultery — the breaking of vows that inevitably results in the breaking of hearts and the shattering of families. But people do not go to hell because of adultery.

Murder takes the life of another person, whether it is the murder of a living child in the womb or the murder of a child by an insane rapist. Do people go to hell because of murder? No, people do not go to hell because of murder.

People go to hell because they reject the suffering sacrifice of the Lord Jesus Christ on the Cross. Let me be crystal clear at this point. The price of rejecting an infinite sacrifice is an infinite suffering.

In short, the pain of hell is the eternal retribution of rejecting the infinite pain of the perfect sacrifice of the Son of God. If you reject what He did in enduring the most excruciating penalty in history, you will go to hell.

Hell is a place of suffering. "And in hell he lift up his eyes, being in torments . . ." (Luke 16:23). The rich man of Jesus' teaching cried out, "Father Abraham, have mercy on me . . . for I am tormented in this flame" (Luke 16:24). The man begged that the leper who lay outside his gate in his earthly life now come and touch his tongue with just one drop of water for that most slight and temporary relief. Jesus paints a picture of total and permanent torture and torment in a place called hell.

One of the greatest difficulties of the liberal theologians who love Jesus but reject hell is the grave truth that *Jesus said more about hell than anyone else.* The same tenderhearted Lord who healed the diseased, gave sight to the blind, gave hearing to the deaf, and freed the demon-possessed was the same Lord who gave the most vivid pictures of hell in the New Testament. There are 1,850 verses in the New Testament that record the words of Jesus. Of these, 13 percent deal with hell and judgment. Jesus spoke about hell more than He spoke about heaven. Jesus said more about hell than did the Apostle Paul. In fact, the lone subject He spoke about more than hell was salvation! He repeatedly gave sobering warnings of the eternal nature of torment in hell. You cannot have the Jesus of the New Testament without His teachings about hell. If you doubt His teachings about hell, you might as well doubt the story of His crucifixion and Resurrection.

The Skeptics and Unbelievers

That said, there have been those who have doubted and still do. Colonel Robert Ingersoll, a well-known 19th-century atheist, wrote, "The idea of hell was born of revenge and brutality on one side, and cowardice on the other. . . . I have no respect for any human being who believes in it. . . . I dislike the doctrine, I hate it, I despise it, I defy this doctrine. . . . This doctrine of hell is infamous beyond all power to express."[11] British-born Bertrand Russell, an outspoken and often-quoted philosopher who died in 1970, wrote the following in one of his many essays, entitled, "Why I Am Not a Christian." "There is one very serious defect to my mind in Christ's moral character, and that is that He believed

---

11. Robert G. Ingersoll, quoted in Carl G. Johnson, *Hell, You Say!* (Newtown, PA: Timothy Books, 1974), p. vii.

in hell. I do not myself feel that any person who is profoundly humane can believe in everlasting punishment."[12] I have often wondered what he thinks about hell now since he most likely went there on February 2, 1970!

Hell: Fact or Fiction?

The person who doubts the existence of hell must deny the Word of God or consider that Jesus was simply mistaken or deliberately misled people. But if Jesus was mistaken, He was not the perfect Son of God, and we have no business believing anything He said about God. If Jesus deliberately misled humanity about the existence of hell, He has perpetrated an incredible fraud on the human race. He does not deserve the name Lord and should not be worshiped if He, in fact, deceived humanity about the existence of a terrible place called hell.

The only other possibility is the invention of hell by the early Church and the fraudulent placement of the teaching about hell on the lips of Jesus. This is the conclusion of the modern, so-called "Jesus Seminar." This outlandish group of liberal university scholars considers that most of the gospels were an invention of the early Church, including their teaching about hell. If this were true, then we could rely on *nothing* in the New Testament. If it were possible that Matthew, Mark, Luke, and John invented stories out of the blue and placed them on the lips of Jesus, there would be no basis for our faith whatsoever. In addition, this would mean that each and every person who chose martyrdom instead of renouncing faith in Jesus died for a lie. There is an old saying that bears a timeless truth: *people may live a lie but they would never knowingly die for one.* Those who sacrificed their lives did so because they had seen the resurrected Jesus and knew He was alive!

---

12. Bertrand Russell, *Why I Am Not a Christian and Other Essays on Religion and Related Subjects* (New York: Simon & Shuster, 1957).

To the contrary, the best evangelical scholars have discovered through painstaking research that the earliest Church carefully treasured the words of Jesus and preserved them with great care. The holy Apostles and the Church fathers treasured the *ipsissima verba*, the very words of Jesus, for centuries. They would not dare change a fragment of what He said.

My friend, you are up against an awesome truth. Jesus taught the reality of hell because hell is a reality. He could not have been the Son of God and the Savior of the world without telling us the truth about the awful consequence of rejecting His sacrifice.

When your heart takes its last beat, your eternity has begun. When you breathe your last breath, your eternity has begun. You are going to awaken in one of two eternal dimensions. You will wake up in the glorious presence of Almighty God and His eternal Son amidst the saints of the ages and myriads of angels, or you will wake up all alone in hell. Yes, I said all alone. One of C.S. Lewis's greatest insights was penned in his book about hell, *The Great Divorce* — possibly the greatest book ever written about hell. Lewis confronts the usual sinner's comfort about hell that all of the sinner's friends will be there. This false thinking makes hell a sort of perpetual good ol' boys' club.

Demolishing this argument, he shows how hell will be a lonely place of people infinitely distant from one another. Part of the punishment of hell will be the loneliness, the isolation, and the separation. Do not expect that you'll be in a great crowd like a sports bar on Saturday night. You will be tormented and alone. I am continually amazed at how many people, especially men, think they will die and go to hell to be with their friends partying. There are no parties in hell!

Your last heartbeat and your last breath will not be the end of your existence. When God breathed the breath of life into the nostrils of Adam, He infused into Adam and into every individual who has lived since Adam, an eternal spirit. The image of God within us, even the most fractured image of God in the most deplorable sinner, remains and lasts forever. There is an infinite chasm between the lowest, worst, most miserable, and most sinful human and the highest ape. Humans are instilled with eternal existence. You cannot will that away. You are eternal and will exist somewhere for eternity. That is part of what it means to be created in the image of God.

Ignoring the Truth

The preacher who speaks or writes of hell is accused of using scare tactics. He is rejected for being manipulative. Liberal theologians condescend to him as if he were a mutated specimen from another era. Nothing could be further from the truth. The authentic biblical preacher who warns people of hell is warning them of a serious hazard. He understands that it would be a tragedy for them to be misinformed or uninformed concerning the nature of eternal existence.

It is difficult for a dedicated physician to tell a long-time patient that he or she has cancer. But what physician would refuse to give the obvious warning just because the truth was hard to hear? A legal counselor must sometimes educate a client with hard truths about breaking the law. What kind of attorney would not warn a client of the consequences of violating the law? An accountant must often warn clients against shady tax deductions or sloppy bookkeeping that could lead to an audit. What kind of accountant would refuse to do this and only say what the client wanted to hear? Responsible professionals in every discipline tell their clients the truth.

As the surgeon general of the United States has warned that smoking cigarettes will likely kill you physically, it is my absolute responsibility to tell you what you do not want to hear. I have no choice in that matter. My calling and my obligation to you bind me. If I did otherwise, I would be like a pilot who knew a plane was unsafe but still boarded the passengers in defiance of what they needed to know.

It is impossible to describe hell. No one has been to hell and come back to tell about it. There are numerous books in print today reporting to tell the story of those who have had an "out of body" or "death" experience in which they visited hell and returned. I am not buying into that philosophy. Why? Because we must never rely on personal anecdotes where there is biblical truth to certify what is said. For example, I believe the story of Noah's ark whether someone finds the ark in Turkey or not. In the same way, I do not have to interview someone who has literally been to hell and back to validate my belief in hell. In fact, Jesus addressed that very point when He said, "If they hear not Moses and the prophets, neither will they be persuaded, though one rose from the dead" (Luke 16:31).

What Is Hell Like?

What is hell like? Is it a literal fire? Dr. Billy Graham has been asked that repeatedly. Dr. Graham responds that he does not know, but that every symbol in the Bible stands for a reality that is stronger than the symbol. If the Bible tells us that hell is fire, then the reality must be worse than the symbol.

Have you ever burned your finger? You know the excruciating pain of a simple burn on one finger. I am aware of a Washington man with over 99 percent of his body burned. People can barely stand to look at him. He cannot begin to explain the pain he has suffered. There is no way a person can explain that kind of pain. It is beyond comprehension. Yet the suffering of hell will be of a burning nature even more severe than that.

Jesus repeatedly used the Aramaic term *gehenna* when He referred to hell. The people of His day understood this term to be a reference to the Valley of Hinnom outside the Dung Gate of the ancient city of Jerusalem. Refuse and garbage from the city was carried out the Dung Gate and dumped into the Valley of Hinnom, along with the bodies of dead criminals, animals, etc. It was a place of perpetual fire and vermin. The stench, the maggots, the fire, and the garbage conjured up the image of a terrible destiny. The gentle Lord Jesus used this to describe the destiny of those who died rejecting His sacrifice on the Cross.

What an awful image! Hell is something of a cosmic garbage dump. What would it be like to find oneself forever in a place of such torment that the Son of God Himself could only compare it to a garbage dump? This is sobering language indeed. In the narrative of the rich man and the beggar, Jesus says twice that the rich man was in agony and another time says that he was in torment.

C.S. Lewis, in *The Great Divorce*, suggests an unusual insight on the subject of hell. The book is a fictional trip to heaven undertaken by some residents from hell. When the men and women from hell arrive in heaven, they find that they cannot stand anything about it. The green grass itself is like spikes to their feet. It is too *real.* The light is too bright, and they complain that it sears their eyes. The liquid water is solid under their feet and they cannot drink it. Heaven is simply too real for them to stand it. That is, for folks bound for hell, heaven itself would be hell. Why should a person who cannot stand an hour singing hymns in church want to listen to a heavenly choir forever? Why should someone whose deeds are done in darkness expect to enjoy a setting where everything forever is done in the light? Heaven would be hell to those whose destiny is hell.

Does God Send Anyone to Hell?

I have been asked on numerous occasions, "Why would a loving God send anyone to an eternal hell?" The fact is, God does not send anyone to hell! God sent His only Son to the Cross so that no one would have to experience hell with the exception of Satan and his demons. God's will and His passionate desire is that everyone would come to saving faith in Christ (2 Peter 3:9). However, we freely make choices, and with those choices come consequences. It is imperative for us to remember that each and every choice, no matter how insignificant we think it may be, has a price tag attached. The question for each of us is, "Am I willing to pay the price?" One either accepts or rejects the mighty deed of Christ on the Cross. God's love for each of us keeps Him from imposing His will on us as individuals with a free will. In other words, the door handle to hell is locked from the inside. C.S. Lewis wrote, "There are only two kinds of people in the end: those who say to God, 'Thy will be done,' and those to whom God says, in the end, 'Thy will be done.' "[13] Please let me be crystal clear — those who reject the suffering of the eternal Son of God will populate hell. He paid an infinite price so that we could escape the destination of hell. If we refuse the infinite price that was paid, there is an infinite hell to experience. The choice is yours. God hangs the heaviest weights on the thin wire of decision.

Dateline: 1999

More than anything in the world, Harold Rhodes wanted to come back to warn his son, Henry. Harold had doted on Henry. He had spent hours playing catch with him. He had showed him how to shoulder a shotgun and lead a dove. He had demonstrated how to field dress a deer. He had cheered Henry on at T-ball games and on the high school football team. However, Harold had not told Henry about the Lord Jesus Christ. He had not warned Henry of the consequences of rejecting Christ. Harold had not told Henry about hell.

13. C.S. Lewis, *The Screwtape Letters* (New York: Macmillan, 1960, 1964), p. 69.

While Harold burned in hell, he desperately wanted to warn Henry about that awful place. But he could not do so. He screamed the name of his son in the halls of hell, but the scream fell on no ears at all. Harold could not go back, and he could not tell Henry. Henry had churches all around him, Christian friends, and like Harold, would have a Christian wife. If he would not listen to them, it would make no difference if Harold could go back.

The devil, as a master of deceit, does everything he can to keep people from believing in the existence of a hell; but hell is a literal state of existence that will be the plight of all those who reject the Lord Jesus Christ.

— TIM LAHAYE
Revelation Unveiled

4

hell: the separation

"Between us and you there is a great gulf fixed: so that they which would pass from hence to you cannot; neither can they pass to us, that would come from thence" (Luke 16:26).

Unlike heaven, where there is reunion and rejoicing with God, Christ Jesus, and loved ones who were believers, hell is separation: separation from everything we have ever known, loved, experienced, and cherished in life. This separation is final! All of us want a second chance. It is deeply imbedded into human nature to desire another opportunity. Every student who has failed wants a second chance. Every gambler who has lost his money desires another game. Football teams are notorious for saying, "Wait until next year." Boxers want another round. Racers want another lap. We do not like absolute finality.

For that reason, humanity finds the finality of hell a difficult concept to grasp. The Bible teaches that our eternal fate is sealed forever the moment we die. There is no second chance in life. When we die, that's it. We step into another dimension and another place. It is fixed and cannot be altered by anyone at any time in any way! It is final!

There is something in mere human rationality that reacts against that. This has resulted in a great deal of creativity on the part of certain theologians. Entire branches of the Christian Church hold to the existence of an interim holding place, a post-mortem spiritual refinery. It is usually called purgatory and belongs to a theology of salvation by works.

The theology of purgatory works somewhat like a bank account. A person who dies with more bad deeds than good deeds may be sentenced to purgatory for a length of time determined by the bank account balance of bad versus good deeds. Additional good deeds may be deposited to his account by living relatives or friends who recite certain prayers or give donations to the Church. Sometimes it is supposed that departed saints in heaven have so many good deeds in their heavenly bank accounts that they could contribute some to the account of the soul in purgatory. When sufficient rehabilitation has taken place, the soul in purgatory enters into heaven.

One of the motivating causes of the Protestant Reformation was the Catholic Church's teaching about purgatory. A certain monk, Johann Tetzel, was raising money for the most recent building program of the church, St. Peter's Basilica in Rome. He uttered a famous line of poetry in Western history: "The moment a coin in the coffer rings, another soul from purgatory springs." In this very mercantile approach to personal salvation, Tetzel sold an exit from purgatory for a departed loved one in exchange for a contribution to the building program of the church. This so disgusted an Augustinian monk named Martin Luther that he protested this teaching and thus began the Protestant Reformation in Germany. Luther found no biblical evidence whatsoever for the human invention of a halfway house for a second chance.

The doctrine of a second chance, based on purgatory, mis-understands the nature of personal salvation and divine grace. Works cannot save you in this life, no less in the life to come: "For by grace you have been saved through faith, and that not of yourselves; it is the gift of God, not of works, lest anyone should boast" (Ephesians 2:8–9; NKJV). Personal merit has nothing to do with salvation, either in this life or in the life to come. Paul makes this clear for all the ages when he writes, "By the deeds of the law no flesh will be justified in His sight" (Romans 3:20; NKJV). If works will not save you in this life on earth, neither your works nor someone else's will save you in the eternity to come. All salvation is by grace extended in this present life.

Those who believe in a second chance do not understand the nature of salvation by grace. God has made you an offer so good that it is a reflection on Him and His character. It is liter-ally an offer so good that it is only made once. That God would send His only begotten Son to die for you is a gift you have only one lifetime to accept. Actually, it would be gracious enough of God if He gave you one day or one month to consider the death of His Son for you. Instead, God gives you an entire lifetime to accept the death of His Son for your sins and the sins of the world. If you choose not to trust and receive Jesus Christ as your Lord and Savior in your natural lifetime, you will have no more time to do so.

We consider this the case in natural human life. Some offers deserve to be accepted when they are offered, or not at all. Sup-pose an affluent man loves a woman who is poor, downtrodden, angry, alienated, isolated, and hateful. He seeks her out, loves her purely, and treats her generously. He builds a beautiful home for her. He makes every provision for her safety and comfort, but she rejects him. The woman in this scenario is akin to the millions who reject God's gracious gift of salvation.

Dateline: 1999

Meanwhile in Hell

Harold Rhodes never believed in anything he could not see. Although he would never have used the word, he was a strict empiricist. The world of religion, art, philosophy, and anything else other than working at the tire plant near Normal meant nothing to him.

One can imagine Harold's surprise, then, when he woke up in hell. He immediately sensed the most desperate feeling of alienation and separation he had ever felt. It was the same feeling he had felt when he shipped off to Vietnam and left home for the first time, but it was ten thousand times worse than that. He felt utterly, totally, completely, and desperately alone.

It never dawned on Harold that hell would be so lonely. He had often thought, "If there is a hell, all of my friends will be there," and he'd chuckled to himself when he thought that. Harold was not close to anybody. What Harold did not know was that C.S. Lewis was right when he described hell as a place where people are always getting farther and farther away from one another.

Harold missed Betty. Little did he know that the day would come that he would look across the great gulf and see Betty and his daughter-in-law, Helen, rejoicing in the presence of the Lord Jesus Christ.

Harold looked around in hell, saw nothing but darkness and felt nothing but heat. But then Harold looked up. His heart — if he'd had one — stopped. Above him in a rainbow of light was the throne of Almighty God. Beside it, he saw the person he had despised in his life — the Lord Jesus Christ. Since Harold was spiritually in hell but awaiting the Great White Throne for his final and total judgment, he had an ominous feeling that he would stand in the presence of that One on the throne. A fear surpassing anything he had felt in his life overtook him. He suddenly remembered the life of profanity, obscenity, lewdness, secrecy, and everything else that Betty had never known about.

Betty had been a rock, the stronger of the two of them. He knew he would never see her again. This thought sunk him deeper into fear and despair.

The extreme horribleness of hell,
as portrayed by priests and nuns,
is inflated to compensate for its
implausibility. If hell were plausible,
it would only have to be moderately
unpleasant in order to deter. Given that
it is so unlikely to be true, it has to be
advertised as very very scary indeed.

— RICHARD DAWKINS
The God Delusion

5

hell: the sorrow

But Abraham said, Son, remember that thou in thy lifetime receivedst thy good things, and likewise Lazarus evil things: but now he is comforted, and thou art tormented. And beside all this, between us and you there is a great gulf fixed: so that they which would pass from hence to you cannot; neither can they pass to us, that would come from thence. Then he said, I pray thee therefore, father, that thou wouldest send him to my father's house: For I have five brethren; that he may testify unto them, lest they also come into this place of torment. Abraham saith unto him, They have Moses and the prophets; let them hear them. And he said, Nay, father Abraham: but if one went unto them from the dead, they will repent. And he said unto him, If they hear not Moses and the prophets, neither will they be persuaded, though one rose from the dead (Luke 16:25–31).

Sadly, there is not just suffering and separation in hell but there is also sorrow. Every moment of every day, although time will cease to exist, the consequences of one's choice will haunt them for eternity. One of the most compelling reasons I know of to commit one's life to Christ is not just the quality of life in the present, not just the certainty of heaven in the future, but the witness and encouragement one passes to those whom they love as well. I've often remembered the lyrics of the popular song of 1974, "Cat's in the Cradle," sung by Harry Chapin, co-written with Sandra Chapin.

> My child arrived just the other day
> He came to the world in the usual way
> But there were planes to catch and bills to pay
> He learned to walk while I was away
> And he was talkin' 'fore I knew it, and as he grew
> He'd say, "I'm gonna be like you, Dad
> You know I'm gonna be like you"
>
> And the cat's in the cradle and the silver spoon
> Little boy blue and the man on the moon
> When you comin' home, Dad
> I don't know when, but we'll get together then
> You know we'll have a good time then
>
> My son turned ten just the other day
> He said, "Thanks for the ball, Dad,
>   come on let's play
> can you teach me to throw," I said, "Not today
> I got a lot to do," he said, "That's ok."
> And he walked away but his smile never dimmed
> And said, "I'm gonna be like him, yeah
> You know I'm gonna be like him"
>
> And the cat's in the cradle and the silver spoon
> Little boy blue and the man on the moon

When you comin' home, Dad
I don't know when, but we'll get together then
You know we'll have a good time then

Well, he came from college just the other day
So much like a man I just had to say
"Son, I'm proud of you, can you sit for a while"
He shook his head and said with a smile
"What I'd really like, Dad, is to borrow the car keys
See you later, can I have them please"

And the cat's in the cradle and the silver spoon
Little boy blue and the man on the moon
When you comin' home son
I don't know when, but we'll get together then, Dad
You know we'll have a good time then

I've long since retired, my son's moved away
I called him up just the other day
I said, "I'd like to see you if you don't mind"
He said, "I'd love to, Dad, if I can find the time
You see my new job's a hassle and kids have the flu
But it's sure nice talking to you, Dad
It's been sure nice talking to you"

And as I hung up the phone it occurred to me
He'd grown up just like me
My boy was just like me

And the cat's in the cradle and the silver spoon
Little boy blue and the man in the moon
When you comin' home son
I don't know when, but we'll get together then, Dad
We're gonna have a good time then

Every moment of every day, we send a message to those we love concerning what matters most to us. The vast majority of Americans are in a mad dash to get all they can and then sit on the can as the saying goes. Statistics tell us that Americans are sleep deprived, overworked, and essentially unhappy. That message has resonated with our families and loved ones to the degree that many of America's youth have simply checked out. That is, they have seen the emptiness of the older generation's lives and have no desire to pursue the materialism that has so driven that generation. Furthermore, they have witnessed that God, the Lord Jesus, and His Church matter little. They don't ask questions; they simply observe. They pick up the language, the values, and the hypocrisy of their parents. By the time today's youth reach their teen years, many are already on the path to self-destruction, addiction, and much more.

One day a parent holds a loving infant in his or her arms and before they know it that same child is screaming, "I hate you!" Nothing hurts as much as watching the child you love exhibit such disgust, distrust, and hate as he or she blame you for his or her choices.

That said, many times the parents are to blame if in fact they have not modeled Christ before their child and taught them the truths concerning Jesus and His word. Many cling to the promise of Proverbs 22:6: "Train up a child in the way he should go, and when he is old he will not depart from it" (NKJV). However, if we fail to train them effectively, we are falsely holding on to a promise that we cannot rightly claim!

Future Story

As Harold agonized in the torturous flames of hell, he thought of Henry. Henry should not come here. He did not want his son in this awful, dark, hot, horrible place. He had a sense that even if his son were here he would never see him.

Harold began to wail in the darkness, "Don't let Henry come here!" He pleaded, begged, cried, and screamed. No one heard, and no one cared. Repeatedly, like a video that had only one scene, he saw the impact his life had made on Henry. Harold loved his boy, and for all those years he had thought he was teaching him to be a man. Instead, he had taught him how to waste his life and die without Christ!

The mental torment was more than Harold could bear, but it was his to bear for all of eternity. Harold remembered each time Betty had attempted to talk to him about Jesus and he had scoffed. He remembered every time he had seen a Gospel tract or a Bible, heard a sermon or a Christian song and thought, "I don't need this." He remembered the day when Henry was only six and asked him, "Daddy, why don't you go to church with us?" Harold also thought about that Sunday when Betty told Henry to get dressed for church, Henry said he did not want to go and he told Henry, "You don't have to go if you don't want to." Betty was very upset but Harold said, "Let him make up his own mind."

Over and over again, Harold remembered. When he tried to look around him, his eyes saw nothing but darkness. When he looked up, he saw the throne of God. When he looked behind, he saw his past with regret. When he looked ahead, he saw only despair.

Harold did not know it, but centuries before, Dante had written the words over the door of hell, "Despair of hope, all ye that enter here." Harold had never heard of Dante, but he was living the reality of eternal separation from God.

Satan knows where he's headed and he knows the everlasting punishment that awaits him there. Now he wants to persuade everyone he can (including you) to follow him to that place of torment. He'll make you believe any of his lies that he can to deceive you into being his roommate in hell forever. If he can make you believe that you will rule and reign with him there, then he'll do that. If he can make you believe that hell doesn't really exist, then that's what he'll do. If he can convince you that hell is a wonderful place, that will be his tactic. Satan will do whatever it takes to stop you from believing and receiving the truth. And the truth is; Satan hates you with a passion! His only desire is to hear your agonizing screams as you share his torture in the burning flames of hell.

— RICK JONES
Stairway to Hell

6
the departure

But of that day and hour knoweth no man, no, not the angels of heaven, but My Father only (Matthew 24:36).

March 8, 2014, was a "business as usual" day for Malaysian Airlines and the 239 unsuspecting travelers and crew as they arrived at the Kuala Lumpur airport in preparation for their international flight to Beijing. The plane itself was a state-of-the-art Boeing 777-200ER. I have personally flown as a passenger on this type of aircraft more than once, and it exudes luxury as well as the absolute latest state-of-the-art technology in both the cockpit as well as the passenger cabin.

The flight was supposed to be routine. Good weather, good plane, easy trip. But something happened that has left the world at large, and specifically the world of aviation, in a state of unresolved shock and mystery. The aircraft lifted off at 41 minutes after midnight and began its climb to the assigned altitude of 35,000 feet. It hurtled through the night sky at 542 mph. While the crew went about their duties, no doubt many of the travelers went to sleep while others enjoyed the service, food, and entertainment. Thirty-eight minutes after liftoff, air traffic control (ATC) in Kuala Lumpur handed off the aircraft to Ho Chi Minh City ATC and radioed, "Good night Malaysian 370." That was it! No further audible communication ever transpired. Repeated calls were made but to no avail. The plane simply, unanswerably, unexpectedly disappeared! It was something that had never happened in the history of commercial aviation. Airplanes have crashed. People have died. But a passenger jet has never simply disappeared!

The families were notified of this gut-wrenching news by SMS. The message was simple, unexpected, and life changing. It read: *Malaysia Airlines deeply regrets that we have to assume beyond any reasonable doubt that MH370 has been lost and that none on board survived. As you will hear in the next hour from Malaysia's Prime Minister, we must now accept [that] all evidence suggests the plane went down in the Southern Indian Ocean.*

No one thought something like this could happen but it did; and it occurred without warning to a group of totally unsuspecting people!

The Lord Jesus Christ spoke of His stealthy, sudden return to snatch away His Church in the same terms:

> But as the days of Noah were, so shall also the coming of the Son of man be. For as in the days that were before the flood they were eating and drinking, marrying and giving in marriage, until the day that Noe entered into the ark, and knew not until the flood came, and took them all away; so shall also the coming of the Son of man be (Matthew 24:37–39).

The generation of Noah and the generation of the 21st century have something in common. They both believe in *uniformity* rather than *catastrophe*. That is, they believe the world will go on just as it has always gone on. They laugh at spiritual warn-ings, sneer at preachers presumed to be ignorant, and scoff at quiet Christians who warn that Christ will suddenly return one day for those who have trusted Him. They continue their round of daily dining, beverage consuming, and planning for a life of marriage, peace, and tranquility. They believe that this round of life, whether at the country club or the bowling alley, will always be as it has been and is now. Sadly, there is a mountain of mis-placed trust in man's ability to solve his and the world's problems and live in peace.

Noah's generation experienced the sudden, sobering real-ity that this kind of lifestyle does not happen in a world ruled by God, but rather one guided by human expectations. Right up until the catastrophe occurred, Noah's generation continued the unimpeded round of normal (however that is defined) life. Then, one day, a reveler felt a splash of water on his arm and then another on his face.

"Maybe we ought to cancel the party and check this out," he said.

"Let's go ahead with the party," his friend countered.

And so they did, right up until the moment Noah entered the ark, God closed the door, and the partiers remarked that the rain did not seem to be stopping.

Turn Out the Lights; the Party's Over

Remember Dandy Don Meredith and the early days of Mon-day Night Football with Meredith, Howard Cosell, and Frank Gifford? When the game was out of reach, Dandy Don would croon the tune, "Turn out the lights; the party's over." In a real sense, the United States of America — land of the Pilgrim fa-thers and a haven for persecuted European Christians and Jews who wanted a new start — has been in a party since the 1960s. Americans have believed that the party would go on forever.

Peace, prosperity, unimpeded economic growth, unfettered personal liberty, and perpetual self-absorption have marked both the modern and postmodern worlds. Yet deep in the hearts of aging baby boomers, there is a growing sense that something is about to happen. And they are right.

In the economy of God, the next thing on the agenda of heaven is the coming of the Lord Jesus Christ for His own. The earliest Christian writers called this the *parousia*, a Greek term that means "the being alongside." Technically, the term was used for the visit of a king to his realm. The next epochal event recorded on the eternal iPad will be the sudden visit of King Jesus to snatch away His Church. The Church has come to call this the Rapture. That word in Latin, *raptere*, literally means snatching something away. For example, a lady is walking down the street with her handbag on her arm and, out of nowhere, a thief runs by and rips the bag away. This is what the Rapture is, a snatching away. The next thing on heaven's timetable is the great snatching away of the Church, the Christ followers, the saved.

The Rapture will have radically different outcomes for the saved and for the lost. For the saved, the Rapture will be a time of inexpressible joy and celebration. Those Christians who have died and been carefully put away in earthen graves or marble mausoleums will find their heavenly bodies suddenly restored to their resurrected bodies. Christians who have died are spiritually present with the Lord, but they are not yet complete without their resurrection bodies like the one Jesus had. Paul makes it clear that the earthly body is not going to last, and while it is suitable for earth with its required levels of oxygen, carbon dioxide, and nitrogen, God's ultimate plan is a glorified, resurrected body not bound by time and space (1 Corinthians 15). The saints of the ages will come forth from seas and catacombs, vast city cemeteries, and little, lost country graveyards. There will be hallelujahs in the air as grandparents, parents, and children see one another in their perfect, eternal, spiritual bodies.

On the other hand, those who died outside of Christ will simply remain bodily in the same dusty, decomposing, and disintegrating state they have endured in the grave. While their spirits are consciously suffering in the flames of hell, their bodies will await the final judgment of God known as the Great White Throne Judgment when all the lost of the ages will stand before God for the final sentencing (Revelation 20:11–15).

It is interesting to contemplate whether the disembodied spirits of the lost dead in hell will observe the Rapture and the resurrection of the believers. In all likelihood, they will. What remorse, regret, anguish, screams of lost opportunity, and wails of dread will fill the halls of hell when the disembodied spirits of the lost dead observe the resurrection of the righteous, saved dead! The realization that they have missed forever the opportunity to experience such bliss will penetrate the stony hearts of the impenitent dead. They will stare into the deep abyss of their own doom, dreading the certain judgment to come. That horror will be amplified as the catastrophe of rejecting Christ settles in and they see saved family members receiving resurrection bodies.

There's Going to Be a Meeting in the Air

Immediately after the resurrection of the righteous dead, the living Christians on earth will experience an incredible transformation. Wherever they are and whatever they are doing, they will suddenly begin to ascend into the clouds of heaven. They will levitate by the command of God Himself. As they are en route, they will find their bodies being suddenly transformed. Paul declares that this will happen in the twinkling of an eye (1 Corinthians 15:52). The Greek word *atomos* gives us our English word *atom* and suggests the least divisible amount of anything. Paul states that in the least divisible amount of time — in time so sudden that it cannot be divided anymore — we will be changed into our new spiritual bodies.

Consider the remarkable experience this shall present. Old men, wracked with arthritis or stooped with time, will suddenly find themselves renewed, youthful, vigorous, and energetic. The Christian quadriplegic will suddenly leap from the wheelchair and experience the freedom of mobility. The blind Christians cowering in some corner will see the bright beauty of the appearing of Christ. There's going to be a meeting in the air! The joy, bliss, ecstasy, and wonder of it defy all description.

The When of the Rapture

There are several views about the timing of this incredible event. I believe the Scriptures teach a Pre-Tribulation view. This view simply means that the event will take place before (hence the prefix *pre*) the world is thrust into the seven-year tribulation period. Some have suggested that those who choose to believe this do so out of fear, a sort of pie-in-the-sky mentality. In other words, they say believing this is comforting to their souls and calming to their anxiety. It is rather strange that they would make this accusation considering what the Word of God itself states. The Apostle Paul says it this way:

> For the Lord himself shall descend from heaven with a shout, with the voice of the archangel, and with the trump of God: and the dead in Christ shall rise first: Then we which are alive and remain shall be caught up together with them in the clouds, to meet the Lord in the air: and so shall we ever be with the Lord. Wherefore COMFORT one another with these words (1 Thessalonians 4:16–18; emphasis mine).

It is comforting and calming to know in one's heart that as Jesus said, "in the world you will have tribulation" (John 16:33;

NKJV), but that THE TRIBULATION (Matthew 24:22) is not for the believer.

In fact, the only position regarding the Rapture that fits with Scripture completely is the Pre-Tribulation position. This teaching fits if one applies the golden rule of interpretation: *When the plain sense of Scripture makes sense, seek no further sense, lest you end up with nonsense.* In addition, the Pre-Tribulation position makes perfect sense when we consider that Jesus likened our relationship to Him as the groom and we, the saved, as the bride (see author's book, *Signs of the Second Coming of Christ*, for a complete treatment on this subject). I ask you, what groom takes his bride, puts her through unimaginable horror and judgment, judgment in which 50 percent of the world's population dies, and then says, "Okay, now I will take you to be my bride"?

That idea not only sounds ridiculous, it *is* ridiculous! The Bible states, "For God hath not appointed us to wrath, but to obtain salvation by our Lord Jesus Christ, who died for us, that whether we wake or sleep, we should live together with Him. Wherefore comfort yourselves together, and edify one another, even as also ye do" (1 Thessalonians 5:9–11).

Others believe in a Mid-Tribulation position. These folks believe the saved — the Church — will be left on earth during the first three and one-half years of the Tribulation. The disciples of this position make a sharp distinction between the Tribulation and the Great Tribulation. This teaching then has the Rapture occurring in the middle (hence, mid) of the Tribulation. I strongly disagree with this. The Scriptures teach that "But of that day and hour no man knows, not even the angels of heaven, but my Father only" (Matthew 24:36). According to this view, the beginning of The Tribulation will be when the nation of Israel enters into a seven-year peace agreement with the coming one-world government (Daniel 2) led by a dynamic leader who is actually the Antichrist. This treaty will allow the Jews to rebuild their temple in Jerusalem and reinstitute temple worship and sacrifice (Daniel 9:27).

The beginning of The Great Tribulation will be when the temple sacrifice is stopped or taken away, and the abomination of desolation (an image of the Antichrist) is erected on a wing of the rebuilt temple (Daniel 12:11). If the saved were on earth during this time, they would know that the day of the coming of Jesus would be exactly 1,260 days. This position violates biblical immanency regarding Christ's coming. Furthermore, Jesus told us we are to WATCH for His coming (Matthew 24:42, 25:11, 13). If we were not snatched up before the Tribulation began, we would be watching for the Tribulation and the appearing of the Antichrist, not Jesus!

A third view is known as the Post-Tribulation view. Some call this the Yo-Yo Position since it has the saved going up in the Rapture and immediately turning around and coming down in the Second Coming. As you might suspect, it simply means the Rapture will occur *after* the Tribulation. This position has the Church present on earth during the entire seven-year period. Again, this violates the immanency factor of Christ's return. If we were present on earth during this period, we would simply count forward 2,520 days (360 days in a Jewish year times seven years).

In addition, this view allows no time in heaven for the Judgment Seat of Christ (Romans 14:10; 2 Corinthians 5:10) or the Marriage Supper of the Lamb (Revelation 19:9). That said, the main reason this view cannot be correct is because when Christ returns, there will be a judgment of those who survive the Tribulation (Matthew 25:31–46). At this time, the lost will be sent to hell, and those who came to faith in Christ during the Tribulation will enter into the 1,000-year reign on earth in their physical bodies in order to continue to procreate. If all believers are caught up and changed, then return to earth with Jesus, there will be no one in a physical body to enter into the 1,000-year reign and continue to populate the kingdom. People must be born in the flesh with a sinful nature and make a choice to surrender to the lordship of Christ during this time. Many will not and will then choose to follow Satan in his final rebellion against God at the end of the thousand years (Revelation 20:7–10). This cannot happen IF we are all in glorified, resurrected bodies!

The Partial-Rapture theory, yet another Rapture position, is a relatively new idea. Without going into detail on this preposterous position, let me say that it is built on shifting sand and lacks a solid biblical foundation. The idea in a nutshell is that only the Spirit-filled, sold-out, dedicated believers will be caught up. The believers who are saved, *so as through fire* (1 Corinthians 3:15), will be left behind to endure the suffering of the Tribulation. The biblical proof for this idea seems to be the passage in Matthew 25:1–13 where Jesus is teaching, using a parable of five wise virgins and five foolish ones. The key phrase in this passage is found in verse 12, *I do not know you*, indicating that these foolish ones are not saved. Therefore, we can say with certainty that to suggest a division among believers is wrong.

There is much confusion today in churches and among teachers, preachers, and the like to the point that many Christ followers have chosen to ignore what Scripture says on this important subject. This is a sad and very serious choice that they have made.

Why is there such confusion, and where does it come from? We know the Word of God says that God is not the author of confusion (1 Corinthians 14:33), but we know who is — Satan! You might ask why Satan would want to confuse this issue. I am convinced it is because if he can cast a cloud over the return of Jesus to collect His followers as Christ promised, we will lose our sense of urgency concerning the truth that it might happen today! We cannot be lulled into a sense of complacency concerning the sharing of the Good News, mission endeavors, and living a life of personal holiness because — *maybe today!*

Dateline: 2003

Meanwhile, Back at the Cemetery

In 1990, Harold and Betty Rhodes had — at the urging of Harold's mother — purchased two burial plots next to Harold's parents. Many considered Restland Park to be one of the most desirable cemeteries in Normal, Ohio, and the Rhodes naturally wished to be buried near one another. This was ironic insofar as their real destinies would be far apart.

Harold died in 1999. Betty Rhodes had paid a fierce price for disobeying the clear commandment of God that believers should not be married to unbelievers (2 Corinthians 6:14). Even though she was a devout woman, she'd felt she could somehow avoid the sad realities of living with a lost person. Harold had been a decent husband, except for his opposition to the Lord Jesus Christ and everything related to His Church. Whenever Betty wished to expand her involvement in her church's program, Harold objected to it so vehemently that she submitted to him quietly.

After Harold died, however, it was as if Betty wished to make up for lost time. For four years, she earnestly participated in the entire scope of the church program. She worked in the nursery with little children, joined the handbell group on Wednesday evenings, and sang with the senior choir on Fridays. In retrospect, Betty came to wish she had withstood Harold's objections over the years. Now she understood the joy involved in unfettered service to the Lord Jesus Christ.

One fateful day, a drunken driver crashed into Betty's car as she returned from the Sunday-morning services. Just as with most people, Betty had not awakened that day with any plans of dying. The Bible often reminds us of its certainty, but as the famous psychiatrist suggested, no man can truly conceive of his own death. Betty spoke her last words at the wheel of her crushed car — "Lord Jesus, receive my spirit."

Unbelievably, in the least divisible amount of time, Betty was whisked away from the scene of the crash and in her spirit stood in the midst of the events described in Revelation 4 and 5. There was no pain, remorse, regret, fear, or shock about the accident she had just experienced, as she was now in the presence of the Father, Son, and Holy Spirit, singing the praises of the risen Lord Jesus Christ along with the saints of the ages.

Betty did not see the aftermath of her death on earth. The ambulance took her physical body to the hospital, where she was pronounced dead upon arrival. Then her mortal remains were taken to Restland Funeral Home. Her son, Henry, and daughter-in-law, Helen, gathered with other family members in the family parlor of the funeral home, where the closed casket sat in mute silence at Betty's apparently tragic end. Helen stood quietly in prayerful composure while Henry wailed, bawled, and sobbed all over the room in an uncharacteristic display of emotion. Just four years earlier, his father had died, and now his mother was gone as well. Henry felt the full weight of his own mortality and an ominous sense that all was not well with him after all.

Helen had often tried to share the Word and will of God with Henry — the fallen nature of the world, the certainty of suffering, the reality of death and eternity. Henry would have nothing to do with it. He usually left the room, opened a beer, and turned on a ball game. Henry even sped up when he drove by a cemetery at night, like a child afraid of the dark.

Henry excused himself to the men's room to regain his composure. When he came out, he noticed on a nearby table a gospel tract entitled, "Got Life?" Just as he picked up the tract, Betty's

Bible study fellowship leader placed her hand on his shoulder. A remarkable dialogue took place.

"Betty often asked us to pray for you at Bible study," the gentle lady told Henry.

Henry felt a rush of fear, dread, and anger welling up inside of him. He choked back his tears and looked into the distance. His dad had warned him about religious people, and he was not about to dishonor old Dad right now.

"Betty so hoped that you would come to the Lord Jesus Christ during her lifetime. She wanted to know that you would be in heaven with her," Dorothy, the Bible study leader pleaded.

Henry turned a pinkish purple. On the one hand, he wanted to honor his mother, but on the other hand, he liked his father's irreligious lifestyle. Besides, he had always felt he was more honest and a harder worker than many of the men down at the church.

Henry politely but firmly told Dorothy, "I have no interest in it at all." Little did Henry realize that he had just sealed his fate for all of eternity in hell.

Future Story: The Next Thing for Betty

After some time, Betty suddenly heard the blast of a great host of trumpets. Then the mighty archangel shouted with a reverberating shout that shook the heavens and the earth.

Majestically, the Father on the throne turned to his Son, the Lord Jesus Christ, and pronounced, "The last one has been saved. It is time to claim your bride." Then, with a seismic force, all of heaven erupted. The moment for which the Church had waited 2,000 years was now at hand. The risen and reigning Lord Jesus Christ stepped out of His invisible glory and onto the clouds of the heavens. In splendor and majesty, power and glory, beauty and light, the returning Lord Jesus Christ moved toward earth — Handel could not have written of it in a thousand oratorios.

The Lord Jesus Christ then opened His arms to welcome home His bride.

Betty looked down on the scene from above. Suddenly she saw her own earthen grave bursting open at Restland Cemetery. In the very act of transformation, her physical remains came forth from the grave. Her now glorified body was joined with her soaring spirit. What a meeting in the air! She now had a body like that of her Lord Jesus Christ. Her eyes were not dim, her feet no longer shuffled, and her mind was as clear as that of a rocket scientist — all in an instant and all because of His great power!

At just that moment, Betty saw Helen. Helen had been caught up from the earth along with all of those who were alive at the time of Christ's coming. Both of them looked radiant. They were 33 years old in appearance, the very age that their Lord appeared to be. They were vibrant, energetic, free, alive forever, and like their risen Lord.

Suddenly someone amidst the thousands and thousands being caught up began to sing, "When we've been there ten thousand years. . . ." The entire multitude joined in singing the old song they had sung for so long on earth. But now faith had become sight and it was really happening. *Gloria in excelsis deo.*

The ultimate tragedy is that all those who end in Hell will have chosen it. Instead of accepting that we are all sinners in need of the salvation of Jesus Christ, their pride condemns them to spiritual death. In the end, someone must be god of our lives. If we insist on being our own god, we shall succeed, but at the cost of an eternity in Hell.

— GRANT R. JEFFREY
Heaven: The Mystery of Angels

7
the divine appointment

For we must all appear before the judgment seat of Christ, that every one may receive the things done in his body, according to that he hath done, whether it be good or bad. Knowing therefore the terror of the Lord, we persuade men; but we are made manifest unto God; and I trust also are made manifest in your consciences (2 Corinthians 5:10–11).

The 1820 presidential inauguration of President Andrew Jackson proved to be the most memorable in history. The great Western hero was an outspoken commoner. He pledged that everyone could come to his inauguration party at the White House. When the day came, he made good on his promise. The aristocracy of the northeast was present. Locals from Virginia and the surrounding areas came. In addition, he had invited backwoods friends from his military days. They all came. They came to the White House in their buckskin and coonskin caps. They spit chewing tobacco on the damask furniture coverings. They stood on antiques. They climbed in and out of the windows. It was a wild, indiscriminate crowd that made the aloof and more cultured horrified. The Wild West had come to Washington. The only way the officials could clear the house was to place huge tubs of punch on the lawn outside.

It is always humorous when people show up where they are not expected. Andy Jackson's party was just such a time. Likewise, Almighty God does not expect everybody to show up at the same judgment. In fact, there will be several judgments in the series of divine judicial hearings following the Rapture. The first of these will be for Christians.

The *identity* of those who will appear at the Judgment Seat of Christ is clear. Unlike the Jacksonian party, only those who should be there will be there. Paul makes that clear in 2 Corinthians 5:10 when he indicates that "we" shall be there. The Judgment Seat of Christ is not the place for the judgment of the lost world. That mixture would lack the appropriateness and grace that will be characteristic of this great, sobering occasion. For the Judgment Seat of Christ is not to determine the eternal destiny of the lost rebels. It is rather a time for the Lord Jesus Christ to review the life of each authentic Christian and to give out the rewards that belong to those believers.

How inappropriate and unlike God it would be for a Paul to stand in the same line as a Nero, a Luther to stand in the same line as those who threatened his life, or a Billy Graham to stand in the same line as a Stalin. That is unthinkable. At the Judgment Seat of Christ, only believers shall be present. Only that is appropriate.

Among other reasons, it is appropriate that all the Church of all the ages gather at one time and place. Time has swept away one generation of the Church after another. The Church militant on earth has never been part of the Church triumphant in heaven. God does not see the mighty Church as a series of interrupted starts and stops. He sees His Church as one great Body through the ages. Therefore, it is fitting that we should all meet to receive the rewards for what was done in service to our King while we were in the flesh.

The living lost world must go through the seven-year Tribulation upon the earth. They have no business being at the sobering business of the Judgment Seat of Christ. Their time for judgment is later — at the Great White Throne. Part of their judgment is to be on the earth during the Tribulation getting exactly what they wanted — a world without the Church and without Christ.

Our presence at the Judgment Seat of Christ is a *necessity*. We *must* appear there. Have you ever received a summons to be considered for a jury? That summons has the resounding authority of a *must*. You may find yourself in real trouble if you do not appear at the courthouse on the day required. Likewise, for every Christian, there is an appearance that is a great must. We *must* appear at the Judgment Seat of Christ. That is a requirement none of us will miss. We may miss church on Sunday or Wednesday night. We may miss outreach. We may miss prayer meeting. But none of us will miss the Judgment Seat of Christ.

That is a divine *must*. The term translated *must* is a word in the Greek New Testament that always refers to a divine necessity. The word reflects something that belongs to the nature of the divine expectation and shall indeed happen. For example, it was the word used by the Lord Jesus Christ when He announced that the Son of Man *must* go up to Jerusalem (Matthew 20:18) . . . to face the Cross — and all that it involved. The Cross was a divine necessity in the nature of the case. In the same awesome "oughtness," it is also a divine necessity that believers appear before the Judgment Seat of Christ. It is part of the divine fabric of the universe that each and every believer shall appear before the Judgment Seat of Christ. For God, it is imperative that every saint come to the place of judgment/evaluation for reward in light of faithful service.

God will be no man's debtor. He knows that faithful saints who have spent a lifetime battling the world, the flesh, and the devil, deserve a reward. He recognizes that those who have sacrificed on earth deserve their moment in heaven. He takes reward for Christians seriously. In a lower, lesser, lighter way, we recognize the necessity of reward on earth.

Just off Interstate 77 at Canton, Ohio, is the Pro Football Hall of Fame. Every year, a few of the best of the best are enshrined there with a bust and a record of their achievements. The nation demanded and the fans required that we not forget a Johnny Unitas, a Tom Landry, or a Walter Payton. It's an obvious *must* that there be somewhere to remember these legends for all they have meant to the game. No one begrudges it. It would be unthinkable that there not be such a place of recognition, honor, and celebration.

If that is true on a lower, lesser, earthly level, how much more is it a necessity on the divine, eternal heavenly level? Shall a Paul, a Wycliffe, a Lottie Moon, or a million lesser-known saints live a life for the Lord Jesus and all of that life be forgotten, unrewarded, and unrecognized? No, God shall have a moment of divine necessity when all shall be rewarded.

I am reminded of an old but true story of a missionary couple who had spent their adult lives for the cause of Christ in a foreign land. They happened to be retiring and returning home on the very same ship upon which the current president, Theodore Roosevelt, was traveling. Roosevelt was returning from a wild-game hunting trip on the continent of Africa. As the ship prepared to dock, the elderly couple made their way topside. They observed a great crowd that had gathered to welcome the president home. As they disembarked, the wife said to her husband, "After all these years of service to our Lord Jesus, no one is here to meet us." As they made their way through the throng gathered on shore, the husband turned to his wife and simply said, "There's no one here to meet us because we are not home yet!"

Some have a problem with the very idea of reward as it relates to the Judgment Seat of Christ. Why should Christians serve God with an eye on reward? Is that a base motive for service? The answer is relatively simple. Consider the following examples. The reward to a student who practices music faithfully is the ability to play more music. The reward to a scholar who learns a foreign language is the ability to speak that language fluently. The reward of an athlete who trains is excellence in the game. Along those lines, the reward of the Christian is more of what the Christian always wanted — the fellowship and service of the Lord Jesus Christ.

There is also a *human necessity*. This vile world is no friend of grace. Christians deserve a moment of vindication, celebration, and elevation for the lives they have lived. Some ask why God would not do that for each Christian individually as they went to be with Him. The answer is settled and simple: the influence of any Christian life continues long after that life is over.

For example, the sermons of Charles H. Spurgeon, who died in 1892, are still printed, read, and preached all over the world. It is likely that on the day of the Rapture, someone somewhere will be blessed by a Spurgeon sermon. Charles H. Spurgeon's reward will come only after the full scope of his influence and blessing on others has been realized. In a lesser way, that is true for all of us. The goodness, kindness, and sanctity of a devoted Christian life has an influence far beyond itself. A mother influences a daughter who leads a granddaughter to Christ, and so it goes through the generations.

There is a *totality* of Christians that must appear before the Judgment Seat of Christ. *We must all appear. . . .* We have all known people who miss appointments habitually. They may be charming, well-intentioned people, but they simply miss appointments. No Christian shall miss his or her appointment with the Judgment Seat of Christ. It is a divine appointment.

Sometimes we think the Judgment Seat of Christ will be for spectacular superstars of the Christian faith — Paul, Luther, Wesley, or Graham. Others think the Judgment Seat of Christ is for those Christians who are saved "so as by fire," a place of rebuke and warning for those saved but without reward. In fact, all of us — every Christian of every age — shall appear before Christ at this judgment. The most common, ordinary, pedestrian Christian shall be there. The deacon and the preacher, the usher and the youth leader, the singer and the pianist, the single mom and the aged missionary shall all of them have an individual time with the Lord Jesus Christ.

Think of it! You will stand before the risen Lord Jesus Christ at His great *Bema*, His Judgment Seat. Most of us would be nervous to stand before the lowest court in our city, a mere small claims court. The thought of standing before a civil district court would give us distress. The idea of standing before the United States Supreme Court is beyond anything we can even imagine. Yet each believer has a destiny more daunting than that. We shall stand before the One who loved us, died for us, rose for us, and sits at the right hand of the Father for us.

There will be no empty chairs at God's great family court. At most homes, someone may be missing from the table at Thanksgiving or at Christmas. There is an empty chair and an absence of someone who, through some necessity, is far away. There will be no such absences at the Judgment Seat of Christ. We shall all be there.

Perhaps the most significant word about the Judgment Seat of Christ is *transparency*. There is the suggestion that we shall all be flooded with light at that moment. We shall be made manifest. We shall be raked over with that light from which nothing is hidden. That light will be like a heavenly MRI, seeing through us and revealing everything within us. For the Christian who loves the Lord Jesus Christ and has put forth effort to live for Him, that is a *tremendous* moment, not a terrible moment. The desire of every born-again believer is to be like Jesus. We wish to be like Jesus all day long, in the shop and in the home. Yet we fail. We fall short. The good that we would, we do not, and that which we would not, we do. When we stand in the light of the Judgment Seat, all of that which impeded, frustrated, and retarded us will be burned away. We will be revealed to ourselves more than to Him. The Lord Jesus knows us, but we shall be made manifest to ourselves and in that moment, "We shall be like him, because we shall see him as he is" (1 John 3:2; ESV).

That great manifesting light will also manifest our true selves to others. There is a great deal of misunderstanding, limited compassion, and harsh judgment even in the family of God. The brother next to us may have no idea what we are enduring. Some always think we should have done better, could have tried harder, and might have achieved more. In that moment, our true hearts will be manifest. It will be shown who indeed loved the Lord. Others will see that we could have built pyramids for God, but we only had pebbles. We could have woven golden garments, but only had burlap thread. How much more would some of us have done if only we could have done it? In that great moment, the truth of our motives, desires, and longings to be, do, and go for the Lord Jesus shall be revealed.

Unfortunately, that light will also reveal as fool's gold what appeared to be true gold for the Kingdom of God. A complement to 2 Corinthians 4 is the great passage in 1 Corinthians 3:11–15. Paul wrote of two ways to build on the foundation of the Lord Jesus Christ. Some Christians build with valuable materials: gold, silver, and precious stones. Other Christ-followers build with worthless materials: wood, hay, and stubble. At the Judgment Seat of Christ, the light of a mighty fire will test the true value of every Christian life. Those who have built their Christian lives with costly materials will receive rewards. Those who have built their Christian lives with worthless materials will be saved like a man running out of a burning building with nothing but the clothes on his back.

The background of this passage was the fire that would sometimes sweep through the Greek cities. The cities were a combination of beautiful marble temples and hovels made of straw. The fire would leave the great marble temples standing, but would quickly consume the shanties made with the refuse of the street. Some Christians have built lives like temples; those lives shall stand the test of the fire because they were built with a lifetime of sacrificial service. Other Christians have lived more selfishly and built very little into their lives. They were saved, but that is all. Sacrifice, growth, and abundant grace were strangers to them. They shall be saved through the fire with nothing but their salvation left. They will have no reward; they will, in fact, "suffer loss." No one knows what that loss is, but the mere mention of it should chill the blood of every genuine follower of Christ. Who wants to find out what it is?

Future Story: Helen Has Her Moment

Although Harold and Henry were nowhere near the Judgment Seat of Christ, Betty and Helen indeed awaited their appointment with the Master at His great Bema, or Judgment Seat. There was no long line with people floating around on clouds like presented in the cartoons. Actually, the worship of the Lamb on the throne continued without ceasing. Betty, Helen, and millions like them had been caught up to be with the Lord. Immediately and consciously, they were in the presence of a great throng of worshipers around the throne. One by one, these appeared before the risen Lord Jesus Christ. There was no dread, only anticipation of seeing their Lord.

When Helen's time came, two joyous celestial beings greeted her as if she were an honored guest. They informed her that they had witnessed her entire life and marveled at God's redemptive influence during her time on earth. Furthermore, they told her that they had actually studied the redemptive power of God in her life; the Lord had sent them to school watching Helen's growth as the primary demonstration of His great power. This caused a gasp of astonishment on the part of Helen.

Then, suddenly, she stood in the presence of the great light. Radiating from the most caring face she had ever seen came a lustrous love. Mouth agape, eyes wide open, heart racing, she stood face to face with Jesus. Her mind went back to the times she sang the gospel song, "We Shall Behold Him," with Sandi Patti. Here she was!

Then He called her by name, "Helen." Great warmth, like liquid love, flooded her entire being. She had never felt so much "at home" in all her life. At once, she was overwhelmed with feelings of security, peace, and unity.

Then He said, "Let us look at your life."

This began a review of her life from its first moment. There she was in her home, with her devout parents, attending Sunday school, visiting her grandmother, and going to school. Yes, there were moments she was ashamed of and regretted having to view with Him. But every time one of those moments came, there was a rush of heat inside the light — like feeling the flash of a fire in the barbecue pit — and those moments disappeared. She watched the morning she had professed her faith in Christ. She watched her baptism. She reviewed every moment of her life with Him. He smiled and often said to her, "Well done, good and faithful servant." It was just like the Bible had said it would be.

Then the triumphant moment came. With His nail-scarred hands, he picked up a crown, which looked like a beautiful laurel leaf with a golden hue, and placed it on her head. When He put it there, she felt more "alive" than she had ever felt. He told her, "Receive the crown of life."

Then, in an instant, she was back with the worshiping throng, singing praises to the Lamb on the throne in the light.

All Helen could say was, "Oh, my!"

The greatest misconception about hell is that it doesn't exist. Just as we believe scientists when they tell us there is such a thing as gravity, so should we believe God when he tells us there is such a place as hell. Many people wonder how a merciful and caring God could send people to such a terrible place. The truth is that God doesn't send anyone to hell; people choose to go there by their own rebellion, and God honors their choice.

— RONALD A. BEERS
& V. GILBERT BEERS
The Complete Book of Life's Questions

8
the world gets what it wants

Future Story

Daybreak in Normal, Ohio, witnessed an unparalleled scene. Henry Rhodes reached across the bed to feel the reclining form of his saintly wife. Placing his hand on the sheets next to him, he felt an unfamiliar void. Henry *always* woke up first, *always* made the coffee, and had done so every weekday and Saturday for the 25 years he had been married to Helen. The only exception was on Sunday, when Helen quietly slipped out of bed to go to Normal Bible Church. Years ago, they had come to a truce. Henry despised Christianity, preachers, and the zany fundamentalists at Normal Bible Church. On the other hand, he adored Helen. She was totally faithful, was always respectful, and had the adornment of a meek and quiet spirit. He had often told himself that if all Christians were like her, he might be one too.

Henry was the foreman at a tire plant. He thought he knew men, life, and work. There was no place in his world for the spiritual or the thoughtful. The nearest thing to transcendence for

Henry was the Sunday NFL game or the time he spent with the boys at the club and on the golf course.

"Helen," he called out. He thought that Helen had gone out to the patio, where sometimes they sat and admired their backyard. Or maybe she had gone out to get the paper. He decided to go outside to the front yard and see if she was there. As he stepped onto his porch, he noticed that Eva from down the street was talking to the teenage daughter of Stan and Marie next door. He went over to ask them if they had seen Helen.

Before he could say a word, Eva asked Henry if he had seen Jake, her husband. As he opened his mouth, Brandy — the daughter of Stan and Marie — asked the same thing about her parents. They were gone from their bedroom. There was no sign of the usual morning preparations. In fact, the sheets of the bed were as if they had not been moved. Everyone stood quietly for a minute, feeling awkward having such conversation but suddenly suspicious of something mysterious.

Then Oscar, the neighborhood grouch and troublemaker, ran out of his front door as if he had been shot out of a gun. He looked up and down the street wildly. Spying the trio in conversation, he screamed, "CNN, MSNBC, and Fox News all say that millions of people are missing this morning. On the interstates, there are thousands of wrecks with no one in half the cars. A plane hit a building in Manhattan on an approach to La Guardia and at least two dozen other planes have crashed."

The trio stared at him in blank astonishment.

The clueless Henry asked Oscar, "Have you seen Helen?"

Eva felt a cold shudder and the deepest fear she had ever known. Her grandmother had taken her to church as a child. The preacher used to talk about a day like this. People disappearing. Planes crashing. Car wrecks everywhere. Eva knew what had happened. She wretched right there on the street in front of her mailbox. Jake was a born-again Christian. Eva was a good woman, but she had never understood what he saw in all of that stuff down at the evangelical church. The trio watched her in astonishment.

"Jesus came back," she croaked out as she grabbed her robe around her and let out a wail that scared everyone out of his or her wits.

Welcome to the first day of the Tribulation. The scene described above will not be fiction. It will one day be repeated all over the world. The world that despised Jesus, did not want His name mentioned in public prayer at the Rotary Club or the football game, ridiculed His followers on sitcoms, and hated His Church will get exactly what it wants and deserves — a world without Jesus and His followers!

We have already previewed what will happen to both the saved and the lost immediately at the time of death. We have even considered the wondrous Rapture of the Church and the judgment of Christians in heaven at the Judgment Seat of Christ. While these events take place in heaven, indescribable catastrophes will take place on the earth. We shall seek to describe in words what cannot be described. There is no doubt that the world will yet experience a time of "great tribulation."

The roadmap to that period may be found in Revelation chapters 6 through 19. These words were written by the aged Apostle John on the tiny fist of rock called Patmos that juts out of the Aegean Sea off the coast of Turkey. John was the last surviving eyewitness to Jesus among the original Twelve. The Romans imprisoned him on Patmos during the imperial reign of Domitian at the end of the first Christian century. Isolated, alone, separated from the churches he loved, and wondering about the survival of Christianity in the face of the power of Rome, John suddenly experienced a revelation — the Revelation. The word "revelation" in the Bible's Book of Revelation is not plural but singular. The book is one united and cohesive unveiling of the final victory of Christ over the might of Rome and every other empire that ever challenged the Lord Jesus Christ. As part of that vision, John saw the events that will transpire immediately after the Rapture.

Revelation belongs to a kind of writing that scholars call *apocalyptic*. This comes from the very meaning of the title of the book, Revelation or Apocalyptus. The word suggests the rending of a veil, the lifting of a curtain, or the taking away of a shroud. Suddenly, the great cosmic curtain was lifted and John saw what could be known only by a direct revelation from God. He saw the great drama of the final victory of Jesus Christ and His Church over all that resists it. A large part of that vision was the events of the seven years following the Rapture. Those events are presented in picture language, in a dramatic code that seeks to present what words alone cannot describe. The great ballerina Isadora Duncan was once asked what she meant by a certain dance. She responded, "If I could say it — I wouldn't have to dance it."[14] In a similar way, God showed John a series of pictures that said what words alone could never say. These visions were recorded in the Revelation.

At the center of the action is a scroll that is in the hand of the risen Christ. That scroll has been sealed seven times with sealing wax. The seals are broken open one at a time, and with the breaking of each seal another horrifying catastrophe envelops the world that is now without Christians and the Church. The seventh seal introduces the deafening peal of seven trumpets, the blowing of which heralds the coming of other catastrophes. The seventh trumpet inaugurates the pouring out of the wrath of God from seven bowls. Like the mighty caldrons in a steel factory shining with molten metal, the wrath of God will be poured out from bowls in heaven — and its

---

14. http://www.dancer.com/tom-parsons/quotes.php.

stinging, burning vengeance will scald the rebel planet that rejected His Son.

Reverent scholars do not all agree concerning the role of the Church in the Great Tribulation. There are those who believe in the so-called Post-Tribulation Rapture. That is, the Church will go through the Tribulation along with the world. The Church on the earth shall experience all of the horrors of Revelation 6–19 during the outpouring of the wrath of God.

Still others have postulated that there will be a Mid-Tribulation Rapture. In that scenario, the Church will go through the first three and one-half years of the Tribulation but will then be rescued before the Great Tribulation of the final three and one-half years. Advocates of that view often rely upon certain interpretations of the prophecy of Daniel.

Our position is that the Church will be removed at the beginning of the Great Tribulation. Among other reasons supporting this, the Church disappears in the Revelation until it reappears at the end of Revelation 19. In Revelation 2 and 3, the risen Christ addresses the Church. In Revelation 4, the Apostle is invited to come up to heaven and view the astonishing worship of the living creatures, the elders, and the myriads around the throne of God. In Revelation 5, the crowned and reigning Christ is worshiped and considered worthy to open the book of human destiny, the scroll that contains the horrors and punishments of the Great Tribulation.

Then there thunders from that exalted setting a cry from one of the intelligent creatures — one of the four living creatures — that summons John and all the rest of us, "Come and see." Those words must have rung in the ears of the aged Apostle John. Some 60 years earlier, on the first encounter with the Lord Jesus, the Master told the first disciples who wished to know where He lived, *"Come and see"* (John 1:39). Now, after all the passing of years, the risen, reigning, cosmic Christ sends another word. That word invites them to come and see the Great Tribulation.

Revelation Chapter Six

And I saw when the Lamb opened one of the seals, and I heard, as it were the noise of thunder, one of the four beasts saying, Come and see.

And I saw, and behold a white horse: and he that sat on him had a bow; and a crown was given unto him: and he went forth conquering, and to conquer.

And when he had opened the second seal, I heard the second beast say, Come and see.

And there went out another horse that was red: and power was given to him that sat thereon to take peace from the earth, and that they should kill one another: and there was given unto him a great sword.

And when he had opened the third seal, I heard the third beast say, Come and see. And I beheld, and lo a black horse; and he that sat on him had a pair of balances in his hand.

And I heard a voice in the midst of the four beasts say, A measure of wheat for a penny, and three measures of barley for a penny; and see thou hurt not the oil and the wine.

And when he had opened the fourth seal, I heard the voice of the fourth beast say, Come and see.

And I looked, and behold a pale horse: and his name that sat on him was Death, and Hell followed with him. And power was given unto them over the fourth part of the earth, to kill with sword, and with hunger, and with death, and with the beasts of the earth.

And when he had opened the fifth seal, I saw under the altar the souls of them that were slain for the word of God, and for the testimony which they held:

And they cried with a loud voice, saying, How long, O Lord, holy and true, dost thou not judge and avenge our blood on them that dwell on the earth?

And white robes were given unto every one of them; and it was said unto them, that they should rest yet for a little season, until their fellow servants also and their brethren, that should be killed as they were, should be fulfilled.

And I beheld when he had opened the sixth seal, and, lo, there was a great earthquake; and the sun became black as sackcloth of hair, and the moon became as blood;

And the stars of heaven fell unto the earth, even as a fig tree casteth her untimely figs, when she is shaken of a mighty wind.

And the heaven departed as a scroll when it is rolled together; and every mountain and island were moved out of their places.

And the kings of the earth, and the great men, and the rich men, and the chief captains, and the mighty men, and every bondman, and every free man, hid themselves in the dens and in the rocks of the mountains;

And said to the mountains and rocks, Fall on us, and hide us from the face of him that sitteth on the throne, and from the wrath of the Lamb:

For the great day of his wrath is come; and who shall be able to stand?

The Antichrist Comes

Surely, one of the remarkable visions in the history of humanity is that of Revelation 6. The Lion/Lamb who is Christ opens one of the seals of the sealed scroll. Suddenly, on the stage of history, there appears a white horse and a warrior rider. From time immemorial, a white horse has represented the conqueror's steed. From the ancients to the famous traveler of General Robert E. Lee, a white horse resonates with the intent to wage war and conquer. The Tribulation begins with the appearance of the satanic masterpiece, the incarnation of all rapacious evil — the Antichrist. The Greek preposition *anti* has two meanings. It means (1) against and (2) instead of. This evil human being will stand against everything Christ stands for and will take His place instead of the Lord Jesus, claiming for himself those prerogatives and titles that should belong only to the Son of God. The world that would not have a real Christ will suffer the vengeance of an artificial Christ.

This figure should be identified with *the man of sin* in 2 Thessalonians 2:3–4. The appearance of this malevolent, diabolic mastermind will follow a departure. There will be a decisive and marked departure just before the appearance of the Antichrist. This departure is not a "falling away" from the faith as some have said; rather, it is the game changer of all — the Rapture of the Saints. Immediately following the departure of the believers, this titanic, satanic figure will appear. Three and one-half years later, he will sit in the rebuilt temple itself and receive the worship that belongs only to God.

Paul reminds the Thessalonians that this glimpse at the end times was part of the basic and rudimentary Christian teaching when he was with them (2 Thessalonians 2:5). Today, some critics condemn the teaching of Christian eschatology as scare tactics or idle speculation. Paul considered these matters a part of the kindergarten instruction given to the Thessalonian Christians.

The Bible ransacks imagery to describe this final, evil manifestation. He is the first beast of Revelation 13, the little horn of Daniel 7:8, and the abomination of Matthew 24:15. In Revelation 13, a ferocious beast arises out of the stormy sea. In the Word, the sea is always the symbol of the chaos and lawlessness of lost humanity.

Major Ian Thomas, a famous British evangelist whom I first heard speak many years ago while living in Fayetteville, Arkansas, once told of seeing a picture on an office wall. There was a hand emerging out of the raging sea. Each of the digits, instead of being a thumb or finger, was a human being. Each of the fingers was in a contorted, angry, and hostile battle with the other fingers. Major Thomas considered it the epitome of lost humanity. We are bound together like fingers bound together on a hand; yet we are disturbingly at war with one another.

Just like the striking image in the picture seen by the evangelist, even so the beast will emerge out of the chaos of post-Rapture humanity. He will be the darling of CNN. He will dominate the headlines of the metropolitan dailies. *Time* will name him the "Man of the Year." The United Nations will crown him the leader of humanity and a peacemaker.

This figure will combine the charisma of all of his predecessors, who were symbols of the Antichrist to come. He will have the fierceness of a Genghis Khan, the wile of an Attila the Hun, the will of a Julius Caesar, the imperial arrogance of an Alexander the Great, the winsomeness of a Charlemagne, the splendor of a Louis XIV, the command of a Napoleon, and the evil intent of a Hitler or Stalin. He will be the dreaded, terrible sum total of every one of his bloodthirsty precursors.

The prophecy of Daniel 9 records an incredible prediction of the career of this monstrous, hideous blasphemer. Daniel reports a period of 70 weeks of years, or 490 years, from the decree of Artaxerxes to Nehemiah on March 14, 445 B.C. By exact calculation, one finds that in the last of those "weeks," those series of seven years, the Antichrist makes a covenant with Israel and sits in the temple itself in the form of his image. One can only imagine the catastrophic consequences of such a presence in the midst of the Israeli and Arab world. After three and one-half years, this disingenuous impostor will show himself for what he is and turn against the very people who enshrined him. The outworking of these events is recorded in graphic detail in the Revelation.

The Horsemen of the Apocalypse

In the aftermath of the disclosure that this great impostor will bring war and not peace, the fiery red horse appears (Revelation 6:4). He brings bloody war in his wake. The history of humanity is the history of waiting for the next war. Ironically, even after the "war to end all wars," the worst war in history took place. War will not stop. No political party or aggregation of nations or religious and humanitarian efforts will ever stop bloody war on a lost and rebellious planet. Yet the worst is yet to come. With the Church absent and the Antichrist in charge, the world will become a river of blood.

In the wake of the fiery red horse will come the black horse of famine (Revelation 6:5). It will take a day's wages to buy a mere quart of wheat — a minute amount. Our food production and distribution system in the modern world is woefully thin. During the Great Tribulation, global war will starve millions and millions. This planet will see powerful men wandering the streets of cities begging for the smallest amount of wheat to ward off starvation. The planet that rejected the Bread of Life will one day beg for bread.

Following the black horse is a pale horse, the spectral horse of death itself. In the wake of war and famine, ghostly death will cover the planet like a horrible and polluted fog. One-half of all humanity will die. If that were to happen in this generation, it would mean 3.5 billion dead. What an awful, ghastly, unimaginable carnage of lost humanity!

The thought of such plagues and disasters may seem far away, but it should not. Middle Eastern dictators have hidden away in secret biological laboratories deadly samples of anthrax, mustard gas, and VX nerve gas. If but a test tube of anthrax spores were released over New York City, much of the population would be obliterated. The same is true of the smallpox virus also being hoarded by terrorists. There is only one dose of smallpox vaccine for every 1,000 people in America. Terrible plague and awful death are distinct possibilities in a world with such malevolent intentions.

Future Story: Meanwhile Back with Henry Rhodes

When it finally dawned on Henry that the Rapture had taken place and that Helen was indeed caught away to be with the Lord, he spent some days in shock. He wandered around their empty house half expecting Helen to come back. Then Henry became angry. How dare God take his sweet wife away in the Rapture! Henry had never liked the God Helen worshiped. Now Henry was angry that God had taken her away. Then Henry became depressed. But just when Henry thought it couldn't get any worse, it did. The news broke that a coalition of Muslim armies led by Russia had launched an all-out offensive against Israel declaring that they would rid the world of Israel and the Jews. Strangely, it seemed there had been a divine intervention and the armies were devastated by a supernatural power resulting in massive bloodshed. Some were saying that God Himself had stepped in and saved Israel! Henry felt as though he was totally losing it. That was when he joined one of the thousands of Rapture Support Groups that had sprung up around the country.

Meeting in a strip center near Henry's home, one of the government-supported Rapture Support Groups met on Monday nights. The federal government had given millions in grants to start such groups. With the massive disappearance of a significant portion of the nation's population, millions were depressed. Schools had lost their best teachers, hospitals their best nurses, and businesses their best employees. Both Henry's supervisor and his best coworker were gone. On top of the stress of losing his wife to the Rapture, Henry had to work overtime to keep his beleaguered company from folding.

A member of the ACLU, a secular humanist leader from the city's art community, led the Rapture Support Group. The group consisted of adults who had lost spouses or family members to the Rapture. They met each Monday to discuss how they were feeling. Soon the group turned contentious, quarrelsome, and confrontational. No one had a good answer for the obvious: millions of people were gone, and God seemed to have caused it. The group only depressed Henry even more, and he dropped out after a month.

Strange as it may seem, Henry decided to go to church. Missing Helen terribly and afraid for his own destiny, he chose to visit the nearby Protestant church. The church had continued its regular round of weekly services without much change other than the absence of approximately 10 percent of its congregation. The senior pastor, who had informed the members for years of the mythological background of the Bible, continued to stand in the pulpit each Sunday. He was not fazed by the disappearance of some of his congregation. He considered it part of the larger context of history and existential existence and continued to give his bewildered congregation quotes from Sartre, Camus, and *The New Yorker*. One by one, the congregants decided he was more out of it than they were and had him fired by the board, most of whose members were still around to fire him.

Then, when things seemed bleakest, events started to look more promising. Henry, who had always read *Time* and *Newsweek*, was entranced by the stories of a new leader rising from the populist movements in Eastern Europe. The man was welding together a huge coalition of people and appeared to have enormous charisma. Everything he said rang true, and everything he did worked. Over the next few weeks, Henry and millions with him were enthralled with the reports on CNN. This majestic man did nothing less than unite all of Europe under an emergency government formed because of the devastation of the Rapture and the short, devastating war in Israel.

In the days ahead, Henry watched the news and read the morning paper with a new obsession. Under this new leader, the New Europeans had negotiated an end to the decades-long conflict between the Jews and the Muslims, and finally there was peace. The darling of Europe had flown to Washington and cemented a relationship with the president. Everything was looking promising, in fact, more promising than at any time in Henry's life. Amidst all of the other remarkably progressive activities, the Jews in Jerusalem were rebuilding their ancient temple. The network shows *60 Minutes* and *20/20* devoted multiple programs to the striking reconstruction of the temple. It appeared as if there would be an unprecedented coalition of religion and politics, saving the planet from disaster.

One Sunday morning, as Henry was about to tune in to *Meet the Press*, a flash bulletin appeared beneath the NBC peacock. The Great Leader was being welcomed into the new temple by the head rabbi of Jerusalem. The venerable Jewish leader suddenly appeared on the screen along with the beaming presence of the Great Leader. To the shock of most of the planet, the Great Leader immediately assumed the place in the temple that was supposed to be reserved for God Himself. The camera panned the crowd as a good number of the temple worshipers fell down before the Great Leader. Henry sat mesmerized in front of his television. It appeared that humanity would have a new beginning, all under the aegis of the Great Leader.

Then Henry saw another news flash from later in the morning that took his breath away. The Great Leader had turned from Dr. Jekyll to Mr. Hyde. As if out of nowhere, a massive army materialized and started a bloodbath. In the days to come, Henry watched as that bloodbath enveloped the Middle East, Europe, Africa, and India. Terror struck the hearts of Americans as it appeared the marauding army would head for the riches of North America. Henry watched in horror as humanity's new darling turned into the great scourge of history. Henry was clueless that he was watching the career of the Antichrist.

The Wall Street Journal had been the first to observe that the activities of the Antichrist (although no one called him that) were beginning to interrupt the food-distribution channels. It came home to Henry one day when he went to the nearby Tom Thumb market and saw that the shelves held only one-half of their usual goods. Panic set in at the neighborhood. Once-friendly neighbors jammed the aisles of the grocery stores, and the teenage girls at the checkout counters broke into tears as people literally grabbed food from one another's baskets. To Henry, it was a chaotic scene out of some science fiction movie.

A month later, Henry sat in his leather recliner in total denial. He had just popped the last bag of popcorn. There was nothing else in the house to eat. The stores were empty and abandoned. The soup kitchens were overrun with people, but not their usual crowd. Brokers, attorneys, doctors, and professors lined up alongside desperate street people to eat some of the diminishing gruel that was passed out to the throngs. Henry had been there, but they ran out of food before he got to the window. So now he ate his last dish of popcorn.

And then Henry just sat there. Sirens shrieked. The city's water and garbage system shut down because the workers were starving. The electricity went off two days later because no one had the strength to show up at the generating station. Henry just sat and looked at the wall. He put his hand on Helen's Bible and wished she were there to tell him everything would be all right.

Henry had just seen the beginning of the troubles. Soon he would understand what was unfolding.

Give me one hundred preachers who fear nothing but sin and desire nothing but God, and I care not whether they be clergymen or laymen, they alone will shake the gates of Hell and set up the kingdom of Heaven upon Earth.

— JOHN WESLEY

9
the final years

Future Story

Little did Henry Rhodes anticipate that as bad as things were, they would get much worse. After the Russians led a Muslim coalition to attack the Jews in Israel, resulting in a massive slaughter, a new worldwide peace treaty was signed between Israel and the dynamic darling of the New World Order.

This new leader, who seemed to come out of nowhere, had pulled off what every American president since JFK had aspired to do but had failed miserably trying. Bringing peace to the Middle East was a game changer on the chessboard of world politics, and it seemed as though everyone was hailing him as the worldwide "Man of Peace."

The Jews had started rebuilding their temple in Jerusalem, and it seemed things were getting better, at least for a while. But then it got crazy! Things starting swirling out of control, and Henry felt as though he had been caught up in the vortex of a great tornado. Everything he had known and been familiar with was changing so fast.

The services normally provided by the city seemed to vanish overnight. No mail, spasmodic cable, Internet, and cell connections. Everything was haywire! The Tom Thumb had closed, and the corner market had little or no food left to sell. When they did manage to get products to sell, watch out. The price gouging was horrific.

As he scrounged the basement of his modest home for canned goods forgotten long ago, Henry sat by the hour watching what was left of CNN. With the failure of the power plants and the absence of the world's best technicians, the network only appeared every now and then. Further, the power plant in Normal, Ohio, only produced power part of the time. Between the downtime of the power plant and the off-the-air episodes of CNN, Henry only caught sketches of world developments. For some of the developments, he only had to look out his front door.

The radical devotees of the Great Leader had developed a curious mark of their devotion; it appeared to be a type of a tattoo on their right hands or on their foreheads. Tattoos had become increasingly popular over the last few years, and while many people had them, Henry had never seen one exactly like these. As best he could tell, it was a mark or a number.

Those who lived near the coast reported that the sea had mysteriously turned a loathsome blood red, and everything in it had died. The red-hued infestation of the ocean soon spread to the rivers and even the underground springs that fed them. The water supply of the world had turned to blood overnight.

As if these miseries were not enough, global warming reached a new zenith. The unleashed power of the sun scorched man and beast with the greatest heat wave in world history. Henry sweltered in his recliner, warily watching the waning water in his five-gallon artesian water tank in the corner of the kitchen. The Everfresh water company had suddenly closed, only able to pump blood from its artesian source. Henry had no idea what he would do when that water was gone.

Nor had Henry seen anybody for weeks. One would have thought the adage "misery loves company" would have driven the lost souls in the neighborhood together. The Great Tribulation had exactly the opposite effect. People were so angry, depressed, and suspicious of one another that they had barricaded themselves inside their homes. Except for occasional runs to the almost-empty store, no one dared come outside for fear of being robbed, beaten, and killed by hungry neighbors. Henry slept more and more out of sheer depression.

Then a curious and strange thing occurred. The Great Leader and his counterpart, the Prophet, had incited unrest in the earth that was leading toward the most senseless confrontation in history. In one of the spasmodic news reports, Henry heard the Prophet announce that all citizens were to present themselves to receive a mark pledging their loyalty to the Great Leader. Henry instantly reflected on his days in middle school history class when Mr. Evans had taught them about how the Nazis in 1939 had made all Jews wear a band on their arms with "Jew" written on it in yellow. Now it was not a band but a tattoo. The report was clear. Take the mark, and access to supplies would be granted. Refuse the mark and well, accept the consequences. Henry quickly headed out his back door on a mission to take the mark!

Then Henry, never one to pay much attention to news and world events, started to notice the escalating tensions in the Middle East. He'd previously tuned out because, after all, it was a long way from Ohio to Israel, and how could the things happening there affect him? Always troubled and increasingly violent, the Middle East now dominated every newscast. Henry remembered the day he was channel-hopping, landed on Fox News (which he never watched) and happened to pause long enough to hear syndicated columnist Charles Krauthammer say in an interview, "There is a general consensus that the world is going to hell."[15] He remembered Osama bin Laden, Yasser Arafat, Saddam Hussein, Ayatollah Ali Khamenei, and others who seemed to put the world on the edge of extinction. That was child's play compared to what was happening now. Infantry and armored divisions from the European Union, masses of soldiers from China, and a horde of armored divisions from nations all over the world were headed toward a valley 15 miles from the modern Israeli city of Haifa. In spite of all the woes on the planet, the hordes of armies from every armed nation on the planet were converging on Israel and the Valley of Megiddo. Henry sat in a stupor as he watched the unfolding drama via the spasmodic availability of the television. The blood lust of unredeemed human beings hurled the planet toward a great catastrophe.

Meanwhile in Heaven

Henry's wife, Helen, had never imagined such a "residence" could be hers, as if the mere human and temporal word *residence* even applied. After her session with the Lord Jesus Christ at His *Bema* — a wonderful time where she had gathered with her Christian family to celebrate the victories of faith in her temporal life — she had been rewarded with a lustrous white garment unlike anything she had ever seen. It constantly shone, but not with some garish Hollywood light. It shone with a gentle, warm light of purity and welcome.

Two gigantic angelic beings had swept her along a golden path to a habitation. *Mansion* was not an adequate word. It was like a great mansion, but utterly different. Every window opened onto a view of the light at the center of heaven and the mighty worship that constantly took place there. The sweetest music imaginable swept through the windows that never had

15. Fox News, *Special Report with Bret Baier*, July 25, 2014.

to be closed because the weather, if you could call it that, was more perfect than the best day she could remember in Normal, Ohio. Many considered the Ohio countryside to be beautiful, but nothing about it prepared Helen for the beauty she saw outside her windows. Even though she was without Henry, she was not lonely. She still loved Henry and knew that he was on earth in the Tribulation, but now she had seen the risen Christ "she had known even as she was known" and was at peace with what had happened to poor Henry.

Then one day — if one could use the word since it was always *day* — there was a mighty and spontaneous movement toward the throne at the center of heaven. Millions and millions of triumphant believers gathered in endless concentric circles around the throne with a myriad of angels. Great praises rang out. The masses of saints from all the ages proclaimed, "Alleluia! For the Lord God Omnipotent reigns!" An electric sense of expectation thrilled the millions and millions. Something was about to happen.

A banquet hall was arranged for an event called "The Marriage Supper of the Lamb." For hours, for days and days, the millions and millions celebrated the life and victories of the Lord Jesus Christ. His eternal life as the Word of God before His incarnation at Bethlehem was celebrated. Then the entire multitude *saw* in review His entire earthly incarnation. It was not like a movie. It was just simply there, before them, presented by the God above all time. When He was born in the stable, the millions of the redeemed cried out "Hosanna!" All of them had loved and read their Bibles and had never imagined that they would be at a great banquet where His entire life — every episode of it — would be reviewed in a great setting of worship and praise. It defied all imagination.

A greater contrast between the despair that Henry felt and the elation that Helen felt could not be portrayed. As Henry ate his last can of ancient and stale corn, the promises of supplies made by the Prophet never coming to reality, Helen feasted at the Marriage Supper of the Lamb. No words could describe the difference in their circumstances.

At the penultimate moment of the Marriage Supper of the Lamb, a striking white horse appeared as if a Pegasus. To the fanfare of a million trumpets, the risen and ascended Lord Jesus Christ arose from beside the throne of light and with the angels as His equerries, mounted the horse. Fire flashed from His eyes. Multiple diadems were on His head. Then, as if under the command of an unseen general, a similar, equally beautiful white horse appeared alongside each of the redeemed, including a startled Helen. In an instant, without effort, she was mounted on the white steed. The horse fell in with the millions of others in the perfectly timed cavalry of heaven. Helen laughed to herself and called it the "Calvary cavalry."

At the head of this mighty army of mounted saints rode the Lord Jesus Christ. The golden streets of heaven thundered with the clopping of countless millions of hooves. Great "alleluias" ricocheted off the parapets of the heavenly city. Wonderment and awe filled each heart as the heavenly army rode behind the risen Lord Jesus Christ. The army was transported in an instant to the vicinity around Haifa. No one knew how, no one cared how, and no one even wondered how. For now, every eye was fixed on the Son of God on the horse, awaiting His next command. Then it was over. There was no battle. The Great Leader, his Prophet, the bloodthirsty armies of the world — all of them simply surrendered. Not a shot was fired, not a bomb dropped, not a sword unsheathed, yet a river of blood flowed 200 miles long and four and one-half feet deep. The Great Leader and the Prophet were hurled into the deep abyss of hell. Demons laughed. Birds of prey gorged on the dead. The Lion/Lamb had won the final battle without a shot being fired. Helen said to herself in her saintly Midwestern simplicity, "Oh, my!"

Henry Makes a Sudden Exit

Henry slept most of the time. The electricity was now gone. The heating oil people had long since been out of business. There was nothing left to eat. There was no water left to drink. There had been no rain in such a long time that Henry could barely remember what it was like to feel the cool drops of water upon his face. The house grew colder. The dog was skin and bones and had eaten nothing for a week. Without electricity, Henry could not watch television, if there was any television to watch. The Internet was down, the radios were silent, and the neighbors were barricaded in their own houses. Not one of the Great Leader's promises had come to pass — none. It finally began to dawn on the depressed and denying Henry that he was going to die — and soon.

Indeed, Henry finally did die. The sum total of the deprivations of the Great Tribulation took its toll on Henry. In some mysterious way, he was further and further away from the life on earth that he had known. A great force propelled him through the universe toward a place of darkness and incredible heat. Even though he was not in a "bodily" existence, he nevertheless was experiencing consciousness, reality, heat, and darkness. Finally, he had the ominous sense of being locked into something somewhere. It was totally dark, unimaginably hot, and miserably painful. The reality of his new home slowly dawned on Henry; he had died and gone to hell.

If sinners be damned, at least let them leap to Hell over our dead bodies. And if they perish, let them perish with our arms wrapped about their knees, imploring them to stay. If Hell must be filled, let it be filled in the teeth of our exertions, and let not one go unwarned and unprayed for.

— CHARLES H. SPURGEON

10
the reign, the revolt, and the renewed world

The Reign: Revelation 20–22

The risen Lord Jesus Christ will reign on a renovated and renewed earth in a kingdom that lasts for a thousand years. He gives us that assurance in His revelation. Satan, the deadly deceiver of the human race, will be chained in the bottom of his own hellish pit (Revelation 20:2). During that time the saints of the ages will rule with Him (Revelation 20:4). Think of it: we will reign with Christ!

There are three primary views of the millennial question. The amillennial view recognizes no reign of Christ on earth for a thousand years. In the Greek language, the letter "a" negates a noun and is the equivalent of saying "non-millennial" view. Advocates of this interpretation identify the reign of Christ with His reign in the Church through the ages. They believe that all of Revelation until the passages on heaven at the very end, applied to the Roman Christians who first read the book.

The non-millennialists further believe that there will be a general resurrection of believers and the lost, a general judgment, and then the eternal order will begin. Dr. Ray Summers, in his book *Worthy Is the Lamb,* presents a fair understanding of this view, and due to the use of this book in many seminaries it is the position taken by many ministers serving God's people today.

The post-millennialists believe that the preaching of the gospel will so improve the world that a period of 1,000 years of righteousness will precede the return of the Lord Jesus Christ. The power of the gospel will transform the planet. Human society and life as we know it will be progressively sanctified until perfect peace breaks out.

In one way this gives great tribute to the power of the gospel. In reality, however, this view is invalidated by the terrible events of the last century. At the turn of that century it looked as if such a thing might happen. The violence of World War I all but killed such optimism, and World War II certainly did, not to mention Korea, Vietnam, Cambodia, and untold ethnic clashes around the globe. The cynicism of the 1960s gave a deathblow to such hopes. A recognized advocate of this view was the founder of Southwestern Baptist Theological seminary, Dr. B.H. Carroll, in his commentary on Revelation, *Interpretation of the English Bible.*

> I believe in the reign of the Lord Jesus Christ on earth for a thousand years. I am not alone. No one less respected than the great church historian Philip Schaff stated:

>> The most striking point in the eschatology of the ante-Nicene age [the period just after the New Testament was written] is the prominent chiliasm, or millenarianism, that is the belief of a visible reign of Christ in glory on earth with the risen saints for a thousand years, before the general resurrection and judgment. It was indeed not the doctrine of

the church embodied in any creed or form of devotion, but a widely current opinion of distinguished teachers.[16]

We should understand some very significant landmarks in the development of the precious belief that our Lord Jesus Christ will reign in the world that rejected Him and nailed Him to the Cross. Even the Jews believed in a millennial reign of the Messiah during the period between the Old and New Testaments. In the Jewish devotional or apocalyptic writings there was the specific belief that the Messiah would reign for a thousand years.

Immediately following the writing of the New Testament, it was interpreted by a group of men collectively called the "church fathers." The Roman Catholic Church has claimed these men, but in reality they belong to all the Church, since Catholicism was not born until the fourth century. For the first 250 years of Christian history, there was no other view in writing other than the expectation that the Lord Jesus Christ would reign on the earth.

One of the earliest was Papias of Hierapolis, the bishop of the church in a small town in what is today Turkey. Irenaeus tells us that Papias had been personally related to "John the Elder," another name for the author of Revelation. In the principal work of Papias, which no longer exists but is referred to by other writers, Papias endorsed the view of the millennial reign of Christ. Now here is a man who personally knew the Apostle John and had the advantage of hearing John talk about the truths he wrote in the Revelation. I believe that Papias should certainly know more about what John meant in Revelation 20 than anyone alive today, and Papias believed in a millennial reign of Jesus Christ.

---

16. Philip Schaff, *History of the Christian Church, Vol. 2: Ante-Nicene Christianity,* 6th ed. (New York: Charles Scribner's Sons, 1892), p. 854.

Justin Martyr (100/10–163/67) stands as one of the revered Greek Fathers of the Church. Justin was born in Samaria of pagan parents. He was converted to Christianity in Ephesus circa A.D. 130. He was beheaded for Jesus in Rome in A.D. 165. In his writings, Justin Martyr clearly championed the view of a reign by Jesus Christ on the earth from Jerusalem.

Irenaeus (120/40–202) stands out as a great proponent of the reign of the Son on earth. He sat at the feet of Polycarp, an early martyr. He became bishop in Lyon, in what is today France, during the persecution of the Church in A.D. 177. He strongly defended the reign of Christ on earth at the end of time. He is a particularly strong voice for the millennial reign of Christ because he was connected to the Apostles through the voice of the famous martyr Polycarp.

Many others could be named, but it would become too technical. Hippolytus, an early bishop of Rome, advocated the reign of Christ. The very first commentary ever written on Revelation by Victorinus of Petau, part of modern Austria, advocated the reign of Christ on earth. Lactantius of North Africa believed in the millennial reign, as did Commodian of the same area. Methodius of Olympus also preached the reign of Christ. These heroes of the Early Church, some of whom lost their lives for what they believed and taught, are bright and shining lights advocating the reign of Jesus Christ on earth.

I mention these for you to understand that the reign of Christ is no modern invention by recent scholars. It was the only view the Church knew for hundreds of years until later scholars began to deny it. I believe that Christ will reign on earth for a thousand years following the Great Tribulation and His glorious return.

The Final Rebellion

At the end of the thousand-year reign, Satan, who has been locked down in the Abyss (Revelation 20:2–3, 7–9) since the

Second Coming of Jesus is now set free for a short time. He then leads a final rebellion against God. This is so strange, is it not? Who would possibly align themselves with the evil one after experiencing a world of peace under the leadership of the Lord Jesus Christ, the Prince of Peace? Yet mankind, in his sinful flesh, those born to the ones who were saved during the tribulation of natural parents, refusing to surrender their prideful will to His, choose to fight with Satan against God. Truth is, it is not much of a battle as God simply sends fire from heaven and destroys the rebellious ones. Satan is then thrown into the lake of fire where he will be tormented day and night forever and forever.

The Renewed World

When the last lost person has stood before the Great White Throne, there will be a fiery and noisy conflagration that will burn up both the heavens and the earth, as we know them (2 Peter 3:10). This will be a firestorm of atomic proportions, which will consume everything. After this purging fire, there will be "new heavens and a new earth, wherein dwelleth righteousness" (2 Peter 3:13). You should note carefully that Peter refers not only to a new heaven but also a new earth. He expected that this weary old earth will be purged in a mighty fire and will reappear in a new edition.

What God does is always incarnation, a downward movement. The Lord Jesus Christ came down from above to a stable in Bethlehem. In the same way, when John sees a new heaven and a new earth, the New Jerusalem comes *down* from above (Revelation 21:1–2). God will not preside over a new order that omits the earth from His plans. Rather, the Son of God will reign in power from the New Jerusalem. What a glorious day that will be when the reign of Jesus Christ covers the world.

Future Story

Helen in the Millennium

Following the defeat of the Great Leader, Helen, along with the countless millions of saints, participated in the enthronement of the Lord Jesus Christ on His throne in Jerusalem. She was thrilled to see Peter, Andrew, James, John, and the others as they sat in great thrones around Jesus. She remembered how different things had been in Jerusalem the final week of His earthly life and ministry. There was no Cross now, but rather a Crown. He no longer wore the clothes of a carpenter, but wore golden diadems of incredible beauty. From His throne, emissaries went out to the entire planet.

Helen wondered how things were in the renewed Ohio. She did not have long to wait. A mighty angel came to her mansion with a scroll in hand. The reigning Jesus was giving Helen an assignment to go back to the Cleveland/Akron area and to administer the Kingdom of God in that area. Helen could not believe her eyes as she was suddenly whisked back to the area she had once known. It was the same, but then again, not the same. Lake Erie, once polluted and foul, now shone with a vivid aquamarine as if it were in the Caribbean. But the most incredible thing was downtown Cleveland. Similar buildings had replaced all its soot-covered buildings, but they were radiantly different. Helen remembered singing the old song, "Thine alabaster cities gleam, undimmed by human tears. . . ." That had never been the case before, but now it was definitely the case. America was beautiful!

At the end of the thousand-year reign of Christ, Helen returned, as if by the speed of light, to her beautiful mansion. There she sat in comfort with the other saints while the awful events of the Great White Throne unfolded.

One by one, those who were in hell, the lost of all the ages, were brought before God for their final sentencing. Harold and Henry were there and kneeled in the presence of God. First, the Book of Works was opened. Then, a voice from the throne uttered these words: "Harold, because you rejected the forgiving blood of Jesus, your works condemn you." Another book was opened. This was the "Book of Life of the Lamb." The final destiny for Harold was sealed when the Lord Jesus Christ spoke these words: "Harold, I came to give you life, a life free from the power and wages of sin. Because you rejected that life, your name is not found in the Book of Life. You will have no part in the new eternity that I have prepared for those who love and accept me." All Harold could do was bend his knee to worship Jesus Christ and confess that Jesus Christ is Lord. Following this confession, Harold, along with his son Henry and all the remaining unbelievers were cast back into the lake of fire, for all of eternity to exist in suffering forever along with Satan and his demons.

As the saints conversed with each other, they prepared for the great fire and noise that would come at the end of the events of the Great White Throne. Suddenly, the heavens themselves shook and roared and burned. All of the saints were untouched by this, with the exception that they seemed to shine more brightly when it was over.

Helen witnessed the coming events by some supernatural ability to see what was happening at all places, for she knew even as she was known.

She saw a new heaven and a new earth. She watched as the holy city, the New Jerusalem, came down from God out of heaven. The beauty of this place was beyond imagination. She wanted to cry, but no tears would come to her eyes. Finally, a voice rang out that filled the new eternal kingdom. *"It is done. I am Alpha and Omega, the beginning and the end. I will give unto him that is athirst of the fountain of the water of life freely. He that overcometh shall inherit all things; and I will be his God, and he shall be my son"* (Revelation 21:6–7). This would be her eternal dwelling place.

Sinners in hell are not the fools they were on earth; in hell they do not laugh at everlasting burnings; in the pit they do not despise the words, "eternal fire." The worm that never dieth, when it is gnawing, gnaws out all joke and laughter; you may despise God now, and despise me now for what I say, but death will change your note.
— CHARLES SPURGEON

epilogue

It's a Wrap

We are all familiar with the words of the motion picture director. After the work is done, after the plan is completed, after the participants have done their part, finally come the words, "It's a wrap!" In other words, it is finished. Everyone who has ever seen a movie knows intuitively when the end of the movie is near. There are signs, certain indicators, which clue us in to the fact that the script has been played out and now it is time to go.

The writer of a novel sits at his or her laptop and roughly sketches out the plan for the story. It must have an exciting beginning, an interest-keeping plot, and a stirring ending. As one reads the story, one understands they are progressing toward the end. The signs are easily recognized.

Life, created by God Himself, has a beginning. I shall never cease to be amazed at how God creates a precious new life, and brings that life into this world only to allow it to begin to die. The moment we breathe our first breath we are progressing toward our last. Someone wisely observed that the wood of the cradle rubs against the marble of the tombstone. The end of one's life has its indicators, its signs. We tend to develop furniture disease — that is, our chest falls into our drawers. We develop the B syndrome: baldness, bulges, bifocals, and bunions. We can recognize time is slipping away.

In our world, while we can readily agree with the above statements, we cannot seem to come to grip with the same reality as it relates to God's eternal plan for the ages. The signs surround us. The Word of God tells us how to recognize what time it is. Yet, for the most part, we plunge ahead as though this movie, this novel, our life, this world, has no end.

Now What?

So, what are we to do? I had hoped you would be asking yourself this question, because I have a few suggestions.

First, you come to grips with the reality that we are, in fact, running out of time. You will want to make certain you know, not just know about, the person of Jesus Christ as the Savior and Lord of your life. The word know in the biblical sense means to have an intimate personal relationship. Adam knew Eve. This was a relationship on the deepest level where nothing was held back. Most people today say they know or believe in God. Yet their lives do not validate this as fact. The question I often ask is, if you were arrested for being a Christian would there be enough evidence to convict you? I have always been of the opinion that the problem has to do with one's understanding and definition of the word "believe." The Bible says the devil "believes" in God (James 2:19), but I can assure you he isn't going to heaven. The demons believe in Jesus and said so numerous times in Scripture. They are not going to heaven either. What does it mean to "believe" in Jesus since the Scriptures teach that the only way to be rightly related to God is through belief in Jesus as the Christ

(Romans 10:9–10)? Perhaps the best way to define the word "believe" is by the use of an illustration.

Walking a Tightrope

Suppose I am a tightrope walker and you saw me perform. You were satisfied I could walk a tightrope. I then posed a question, "Do you *believe* I can walk the tightrope?"

You would naturally say, "Yes, I believe you can walk the tightrope, I saw you do it with my own two eyes."

However, what if I said to you, "If you *believe* I can walk the rope, get on my back and let me take you for a walk." Whoa! Wait just a minute! Now we are talking about something entirely different. We are talking about your believing to the degree where action is taken. That's it. Now you are getting it. To believe is not to utter a word or phrase with your lips. Rather *to believe* demands action on one's part. It means to demonstrate through action. To believe in Jesus means I trust in Him and Him alone for my salvation. In addition, I know Him and there is a relationship with God. That belief is demonstrated daily in my life by how I live. Please be certain you know God, not just know about Him, but know Him through the living Lord Jesus Christ.

How do we know Him? The Bible tells us:

> If you declare with your mouth, "Jesus is Lord," and believe in your heart that God raised him from the dead, you will be saved. For it is with your heart that you believe and are justified, and it is with your mouth that you profess your faith and are saved (Romans 10:9–10; NIV).

We declare with our mouth simply by praying to Jesus and asking for His forgiveness of our sin that separates us from Him! If you have never believed and trusted Christ, why not do it NOW!

Secondly, you will want to be certain that everyone you love and care about knows the "Good News" of Jesus. There is no way we can keep the news of forgiveness and restoration to ourselves. We want to give it away to our loved ones, even if they are not receptive. This is often the case. It is often said that the hardest people to talk to about Jesus are our loved ones. Why? Because they know us and they know we aren't perfect. In addition, they fail to understand that when we were born again into God's family we didn't get perfect; we got forgiven. It's hard for unsaved folks to realize that as a follower of Jesus our lives are "under construction." In our obedience, God is working to shape us into the image of Jesus, and that task will take the rest of our earthly lives. But let me hasten to add, if you do not care for the soul of your loved one, it is doubtful anyone else will. Therefore, I believe we have the responsibility to do all within our power under the anointing of God's Holy Spirit to reach those we love. If we will model the love, forgiveness, and joy found in Christ, it will create a hunger in their soul.

Prayer and the Armor of God

I want to suggest how to effectively pray for our loved ones. First, we must understand there is a spiritual battle being fought over the souls of all people. If you do not believe every person who dies without Jesus steps into a literal hell, you will never be a true prayer warrior. Once we accept this truth, we then begin to understand what the Scriptures mean:

> For though we live in the world, we do not wage war as the world does. The weapons we fight with are not the weapons of the world. On the contrary, they have divine power to demolish strongholds. We demolish arguments and every pretension that sets itself up against the knowledge of God, and we take captive every thought to make it obedient to Christ (2 Corinthians

10:3–5). The Word of God tells us we have weapons with which to fight, but that they are unconventional. They are spiritual weapons. These spiritual weapons are used to virtually tear down strongholds that have been built up in the lives of our loved ones. What are strongholds and how are they torn down? Strongholds are those areas of our lives where we have allowed the devil to gain access. In many cases, these areas are pride, sexual addiction, fantasies, love of material things, quest for fame, acceptance, or any number of things. God informs us that it is these strongholds that keep one from coming to Jesus. However, we can fight against these and demolish them through intercessory prayer. This is the weapon of our faith against which no person can stand, including Satan and the demons of hell.

How do we fight the devil? The answer to this is also found in the Scriptures:

> Finally, be strong in the Lord and in his mighty power. Put on the full armor of God so that you can take your stand against the devil's schemes. For our struggle is not against flesh and blood, but against the rulers, against the authorities, against the powers of this dark world and against the spiritual forces of evil in the heavenly realms. Therefore put on the full armor of God, so that when the day of evil comes, you may be able to stand your ground, and after you have done everything, to stand. Stand firm then, with the belt of truth buckled around your waist, with the breastplate of righteousness in place, and with your feet fitted with the readiness that comes from the gospel of peace. In addition to all this, take up the shield of faith, with which you can extinguish all the flaming arrows of the evil one. Take the

helmet of salvation and the sword of the Spirit, which is the word of God. And pray in the Spirit on all occasions with all kinds of prayers and requests. With this in mind, be alert and always keep on praying for all the Lord's people (Ephesians 6:10–18; NIV).

Here we learn that the warfare is prayer. The enemy is the devil. The objective is the stronghold in one's life. The strategy for victory is the armor of God. But, we must first be willing to fight. That is, we must care enough to engage the enemy. Many simply do not have the will, the resolve, to fight. We then must clothe ourselves with the armor of God. This is difficult, and here's why. We cannot put on the armor of God unless we ourselves are spiritually clean before God. This means we must allow God to shine His searchlight into our life and come clean about areas that are not in line with His objective, that is, becoming like Him. Scripture says, *"If we confess our sins, he is faithful and just and will forgive us our sins and purify us from all unrighteousness"* (1 John 1:9). God cannot fight through a dirty vessel. Once we are clean, we can then go to battle clothed in truth.

The first step is to ask God to reveal to us the particular stronghold that is keeping our loved one from Him. If we are serious about this and seek an answer from God, He will speak to our heart and supernaturally reveal the stronghold. Once this is identified, we then begin to apply scriptural truth to stand against it. That is, we search for Scripture to use against the stronghold, just as Jesus did when tempted in the wilderness (Luke 4:1–13) and we pray this scripture in behalf of our loved one. For example, if God reveals that a spirit of pride is the main stronghold, we can pray the following:

Dear Lord, your word says you hate pride and arrogance (Proverbs 8:13). That pride only breeds quarrels (Proverbs 13:10). That pride goes before destruction

(Proverbs 16:18). That the cravings of a sinful man, the lust of his eyes and the boasting of what he has and does, come not from the Father but from the world (1 John 2:16). Therefore, in the strong and powerful name of Jesus, I tear down this barrier of pride and demand that it depart from my loved one.

This is how we use the weapon of Scripture to tear down strongholds. Most people pray and ask God to save their loved one not understanding God is not the problem! He died for your loved one. Your loved one is the problem. Will the loved one embrace Jesus? He or she may not; there are no guarantees. However, once they are set free from the spiritual bondage of the enemy, there is every reason to believe and claim them for the kingdom of God.

Once we are clean, once we have engaged in spiritual warfare, then it is time to boldly witness in a spirit of love. As we listen to God speak to our hearts, we will hear Him say it is time to GO. There comes a time when we must put legs to our prayers. Let me illustrate. Several years ago, my wife, Sandra came to me and said she felt it was time to go and visit a certain member of her family who lived out of state. She had been engaging in intercessory prayer for some months and now God said GO. She went, not knowing how she would be received, but in obedience and love. She phoned me within 24 hours to share the exciting news of how her loved one had trusted Christ and been born again. It doesn't always work like this, but in the last few years we have now seen 28 (as of this writing) of our unsaved loved ones trust Jesus as their Lord and Savior. Why do we pray? Why do we go? Because Jesus is coming and time is running out.

The Day, the Hour, When?

The year was 1840 and William Miller, a New York farmer turned Baptist preacher, was preaching that Jesus was coming soon. He went so far as to begin to teach that he knew when Jesus was coming again. It seems that preacher Miller had read Daniel 8:14 and interpreted the statement regarding 2,300 evenings and mornings to be 2,300 years. He then concluded that Christ would return sometime between March 21, 1843, and March 21, 1844.

To preacher Miller's credit, he did not pinpoint a precise day or hour, but did narrow it down to a 12-month window. There were many who accepted Miller's teaching and became enthusiastic followers of this teaching. Sadly enough, March 21, 1844, came and went and Jesus did not come as Miller had predicted. Stories abound about how some of the Millerites quit their jobs and donned white robes. Further, they ascended up the mountains and awaited the coming of Jesus, only to be sadly disappointed. Samuel Snow, however, a follower of Miller's teaching, injected new life into this when he suggested there had been an error in calculating and the real date would now be October 22, 1844. This date also came and went and this event has now become known as THE GREAT DISAPPOINTMENT of 1844. Many went away completely disillusioned. Some abandoned the faith and returned to lives of sin while others remained faithful to Christ and realized, whether He returned physically in their lifetime or not, they would someday be with Him for He would come for them in death.

William Miller is not alone. Many throughout the last 2,000 years have sought to announce the return of Jesus. Because of this, many have decided that they want no part of Bible prophecy and have chosen to ignore this wealth of vital information. How sad! I believe these prophetic truths are the single greatest motivational truths contained in the Holy Scriptures. Prophecy motivates us to be holy, to pray, to witness, to give, to serve and to strive to be all Christ wants us to be, because He is coming at any moment.

Today, we have every reason to believe we are living in the final days. I believe Jesus is coming! But, whether He comes today, tomorrow, next week, next month, next year, or not in my lifetime, it's okay. Why? Because whenever He comes, I will see Him, for I am His and He is mine. In the end, it's a sure thing!

And I looked, and behold a pale horse:
and his name that sat on him was
Death, and Hell followed with him.
— REVELATIONS 6:8

Timeline

Church Age

Rapture

Death of America

Islamic invasion

Birth of New World Order

Appearing of Antichrist

Peace treaty with Israel

Antichrist appears to die

Rebuilding of Temple

Peace treaty broken

Image in Temple

2 witnesses killed in Jerusalem

Many Jews flee to safety

Some nations rebel

God's judgment intensifies

Armageddon

Second Coming

Antichrist rules by deceit

144,000 witnesses get the gospel to the world

Antichrist rules by force

3½ years (1,260 days)

3½ years (1,260 days)

7 years / 70th Week of Daniel (2,520 days)

Selected Glossary of Terms

Heaven: The best definition of heaven is simply that this is where God the Father, God the Son, and the Holy Spirit (three, yet one) are. We will not be disembodied spirits on a cloud strumming a harp as many think. Rather, we will have a body suited to the heavenly environment just as we have an earthly body suited for earth's atmosphere.

The only reliable source for what heaven is like is not to be found in the stories or statements spoken or written by others but rather in the Word of God. Who can tell us about heaven except the One who has been there. Jesus and the New Testament spoke a great deal about heaven, as did a number of the biblical writers. But perhaps our best view of heaven comes from the Book of Revelation itself. Revelation chapters 4 and 5 give us a detailed view of what the Apostle John saw when he was transported into heaven. There was a throne with God the Father seated upon it surrounded by 24 lesser thrones upon which sat 24 elders. We discover the 24 elders represent the 12 tribes of Israel and the 12 Apostles. This becomes clear from Revelation 21:12–14. In addition, we find four living creatures, literally burning ones who never cease to cry, "Holy, holy, holy, is the Lord God Almighty who was, and is, and is to come!" (Revelation 4:8). Further, we discover the Lamb that was slain before the foundation of the world, the Lord Jesus Christ, who alone is worthy to take the scroll from the hand of the Father that represents the title deed to the earth. In addition, Revelation 21 gives a further glimpse of the new heaven and the new earth. This is the restoration of all that was lost in Genesis 1 and now reclaimed for all eternity and will be our new heavenly home. I have read no accounts of anyone who has supposedly been to heaven and back that differs from the biblical account.

Please see Dr. John MacArthur's article for additional helpful information: http://www.gty.org/blog/B140428

Hell: The Bible teaches that hell is a part of the abode of the dead known in Scripture as *sheol*. The word translated as hell is the Greek word *hades*. Hades was the lower part of sheol, while the upper part was known as *paradise*. Prior to the death and Resurrection of Jesus, when a person died their spirit went to either hades or paradise. Hades is a place of suffering and torment until the time of the Great White Throne judgment of Revelation 20:11–15 when all unbelievers are judged "according to their works" since they have rejected salvation by grace. This judgment will bring the final sentencing for all eternity in the lake of fire. Here Satan, the Antichrist, the false prophet, and all the demons will spend eternity. On the other hand, when Jesus ascended to heaven he emptied out paradise and took all to "the Father's house" in order that they would be where He is fulfilling His promise of John 14:1–3. Today, when an unbeliever dies they go to hades to await their final judgment, but believers go straight to the Father's house to be in the presence of Christ Jesus the Lord.

Purgatory: This term is not found in the Bible but is commonly taught due to a misunderstanding of Scripture. The idea that a person can, through lighting candles, saying prayers, or any other religious acts, virtually contribute to one's eternal destiny is unbiblical. Each and every individual is created with a free will, and as such has the privilege and responsibility of choice. One can choose to come to terms with their own sin nature, acknowledge their sin, and turn to Christ Jesus for salvation, or choose to attempt to earn standing with God via their works. However, once physical death occurs, one's eternal destiny is sealed and is unalterable. Please remember, the choice is ours and ours alone. No one bears responsibility for eternity but the individual per his or her choice.

Rapture: While the English word *rapture* does not appear in the Bible, the Greek word certainly does. The word is *harpazo*.

It means to "snatch away" or "catch up." I know of no scholar who denies there have been and will be a coming of Jesus for His followers fulfilling His promise of John 14:1–3. "Do not let your hearts be troubled. You believe in God; believe also in me. My Father's house has many rooms; if that were not so, would I have told you that I am going there to prepare a place for you? And if I go and prepare a place for you, I will come back and take you to be with me that you also may be where I am" (NIV). The Bible records six raptures that have already taken place, i.e., Enoch, Elijah, Isaiah, Jesus, Paul, and John, and two more to come; all believers and two witnesses of Revelation 11. The question largely has to do with the timing of the event.

Theistic Evolution: This term is one of many attempts to foster an alternative view of creation upon the world that allows for millions of years. Theistic evolution, day-age view, gap theory, local flood view, framework hypothesis, and progressive evolution are all attempts to reconcile the biblical account with so-called, modern science. The biblical account of the creation being completed in six literal days was accepted for the first 18 centuries of church history. However in the last 200 years this has changed. Theistic evolution describes a belief that God (theos) used the process of evolution to create the world over millions of years.

Terry Mortenson, in *The New Answers Book 1,* writes about the greatly increasing number of young-earth creationists, including many scientists, who hold to the biblical, traditional view of Scripture, and lists nine reasons Christians should not accept the millions-of-years theory.[17] I have included, with permission, these reasons here for your understanding.

---

17. Ken Ham, editor, *The New Answers Book 1,* "Why Shouldn't Christians Accept Millions of Years?" by Terry Mortenson (Green Forest, AR: Master Books, 2006), p. 25–30.

1. **The Bible clearly teaches that God created in six literal days a few thousand years ago.** The Hebrew word for *day* in Genesis 1 is *yom*. In the vast majority of its uses in the Old Testament it means a literal day; and where it doesn't, the context makes it clear. Further the word "day" is used 2,301 times in the Old Testament. Why only question, as unbelieving scientists do, only Genesis?

2. **The context of Genesis 1 clearly shows that the days of creation were literal days.** First, *yom* is defined the first time it is used in the Bible (Genesis 1:4–5) in its two literal senses: the light portion of the light/dark cycle and the whole light/dark cycle. Second, *yom* is used with evening and morning. Everywhere these two words are used in the Old Testament, either together or separately and with or without *yom* in the context, they always mean a literal evening or morning of a literal day. Third, *yom* is modified with a number: one day, second day, third day, etc., which everywhere else in the Old Testament indicates literal days. Fourth, *yom* is defined literally in Genesis 1:14 in relation to the heavenly bodies.

3. **The genealogies of Genesis 5 and 11 make it clear that the creation days happened only about 6,000 years ago.** It is transparent from the genealogies of Genesis 5 and 11 (which give very detailed chronological information, unlike the clearly abbreviated genealogy in Matthew 1) and other chronological information in the Bible that the creation week took place only about 6,000 years ago.

4. **Exodus 20:9–11 blocks all attempts to fit millions of years into Genesis 1.** "Six days you shall labor and do all your work, but the seventh day is a Sabbath to

the LORD your God. On it you shall not do any work, you, or your son, or your daughter, your male servant, or your female servant, or your livestock, or the sojourner who is within your gates. For in six days the LORD made heaven and earth, the sea, and all that is in them, and rested on the seventh day. Therefore the LORD blessed the Sabbath day and made it holy." This passage gives the reason for God's command to Israel to work six days and then take a Sabbath rest. *Yom* is used in both parts of the commandment. If God meant that the Jews were to work six days because He created over six long periods of time, He could have said that using one of three indefinite Hebrew time words. He chose the only word that means a literal day, and the Jews understood it literally (until the idea of millions of years developed in the early 19th century). For this reason, the day–age view or framework hypothesis must be rejected. The gap theory or any other attempt to put millions of years before the six days are also false because God says that in six days he made the heaven and the earth and the sea and all that is in them. So he made everything in those six literal days and nothing before the first day.

5. **Noah's Flood washes away millions of years.** The evidence in Genesis 6–9 for a global catastrophic flood is overwhelming. For example, the Flood was intended to destroy not only all sinful people but also all land animals and birds and the surface of the earth, which only a global flood could accomplish. The ark's purpose was to save two of every kind of land animal and bird (and seven of some) to repopulate the earth after the Flood. The ark was totally unnecessary if the Flood was only local. People, animals, and birds could have

migrated out of the flood zone before it occurred, or the zone could have been populated from creatures outside the area after the Flood. The catastrophic nature of the Flood is seen in the nonstop rain for at least 40 days, which would have produced massive erosion, mudslides, hurricanes, etc. The Hebrew words translated "the fountains of the great deep burst forth" (Genesis 7:11) clearly point to tectonic rupturing of the earth's surface in many places for 150 days, resulting in volcanoes, earthquakes, and tsunamis. Noah's Flood would produce exactly the kind of complex geological record we see worldwide today: thousands of feet of sediments clearly deposited by water and later hardened into rock and containing billions of fossils. If the year–long Flood is responsible for most of the rock layers and fossils, then those rocks and fossils cannot represent the history of the earth over millions of years, as evolutionists claim.

6. **Jesus was a young–earth creationist.** Jesus consistently treated the miracle accounts of the Old Testament as straightforward, truthful, historical accounts. He continually affirmed the authority of Scripture over man's ideas and traditions. In Mark 10:6 we have the clearest statement showing that Jesus was a young–earth creationist. He teaches that Adam and Eve were made at the "beginning of creation," not billions of years after the beginning, as would be the case if the universe were really billions of years old. So, if Jesus was a young-earth creationist, how can his faithful followers have any other view?

7. **Belief in millions of years undermines the Bible's teaching on death and on the character of God.** Genesis 1 says six times that God called the creation

" good," and when He finished creation on day 6, he called everything "very good." Man and animals and birds were originally vegetarian (Genesis 1:29–30, plants are not "living creatures," as people and animals are, according to Scripture). But Adam and Eve sinned, resulting in the judgment of God on the whole creation. Instantly, Adam and Eve died spiritually, and after God's Curse they began to die physically. The serpent and Eve were changed physically and the ground itself was cursed (Genesis 3:14–19). The whole creation now groans in bondage to corruption, waiting for the final redemption of Christians (Romans 8:19–25) when we will see the restoration of all things (Acts 3:21; Colossians 1:20) to a state similar to the pre–Fall world, when there will be no more carnivorous behavior (Isaiah 11:6–9) and no disease, suffering, or death (Revelation 21:3–5), because there will be no more Curse (Revelation 22:3). To accept millions of years of animal death before the creation and Fall of man contradicts and destroys the full redemptive work of Christ. It also makes God into a bumbling, cruel creator who uses disease, natural disasters, and extinctions to mar His creative work, without any moral cause, but still calls it all "very good."

8. **The idea of millions of years did not come from the scientific facts.** This idea of long ages was developed by deistic and atheistic geologists in the late 18th and early 19th centuries. These men used anti-biblical philosophical and religious assumptions to interpret the geological observations in a way that plainly contradicted the biblical account of creation, the Flood, and the age of the earth. Most church leaders and scholars quickly compromised using the gap theory, day-age

view, local flood view, etc. to try to fit "deep time" into the Bible. But they did not understand the geological arguments and they did not defend their views by careful Bible study. The "deep time" idea flows out of naturalistic assumptions, not scientific observations.

9. **Radiometric dating methods do not prove millions of years.** Radiometric dating was not developed until the early 20th century, by which time virtually the whole world had already accepted the millions of years. For many years, creation scientists have cited numerous examples in the published scientific literature of these dating methods clearly giving erroneous dates (e.g., a date of millions of years for lava flows that occurred in the past few hundred years or even decades). In recent years, creationists in the RATE project have done experimental, theoretical, and field research to uncover more such evidence (e.g., diamonds and coal, which the evolutionists say are millions of years old, were dated by carbon–14 to be only thousands of years old) and to show that decay rates were orders of magnitude faster in the past, which shrinks the millions of years to thousands of years, confirming the Bible.

These are just some of the reasons why we believe that the Bible is giving us the true history of the world. God's Word must be the final authority on all matters about which it speaks — not just the moral and spiritual matters, but also its teachings that bear on history, archaeology, and science.

What is it stake here is the authority of Scripture, the character of God, the doctrine of death, and the very foundation of the gospel. If the early chapters of Genesis are not true literal history, then faith in the rest of the Bible is undermined, including its teaching about salvation and morality.

Tribulation: This term speaks of a specified period of 7 biblical years of 360 days per year or 2,520 days according to the Jewish lunar calendar of 12 months of 30 days each. The Book of Daniel gives the specifics as recorded in chapter 9 verses 24–27 concerning Daniel's vision of the Prophecy of Weeks although the tribulation is a common teaching throughout the Bible. The teaching concerns a specific period of 70 weeks (Hebrew-sabuim or sevens). John Walvoord, one of the best-known dispensationalist interpreters, writes in his commentary on Daniel regarding the term: "The English word 'weeks' is misleading as the Hebrew is actually the plural of the word for seven, without specifying whether it is days, months, or years." On this basis, Walvoord and others use the rendering "sevens" in place of the time-honored translation "weeks" in Daniel 9:24–26.[182]

This 70 weeks of years (Hebrew idiom) is a 490-year panoramic view of the end times beginning with a decree to rebuild the city of Jerusalem. This decree was issued by the Persian ruler Artaxerxes 1 on March 14, 445 B.C. and 483 years later Jesus; the Messiah was killed leaving one final 7-year period, hence the Tribulation. See this author's book, *It Could Happen Tomorrow,* for a full treatment of this subject or order his 4-part CD teaching series, *Signs of the Times*, for detailed explanation).

---

18. John Walvoord, *Daniel: The Key to Prophetic Revelation* (Chicago, IL: Moody, 1971), p. 219.

Gary Frazier is a speaker and writer on the subject of Bible prophecy, the Middle East, and current events, and speaks in approximately 40 churches annually. He is a former pastor and has traveled to Israel more than 160 times since 1971. Gary has personally met with every Israeli prime minister since Menachem Begin, with the exception of Benjamin Netanyahu.

Gary is founder of Discovery Missions International located in the Dallas-Ft. Worth metro area. He currently serves as teaching associate at Prestonwood Baptist Church in Plano, Texas, and has also served as an adjunct professor at Liberty University in Lynchburg, Virginia.

Gary's educational background includes Criswell College, Southwestern Seminary, and Louisiana Baptist University. He has also been honored with a Doctor of Humanities degree from Liberty University in Lynchburg, Virginia, as well as a Doctor of Divinity degree from International Bible College and Seminary in Plymouth, Florida.

He has appeared on numerous documentaries and television programs such as the History Channel's *God vs. Satan* and *The Apocalypse Code*, as well as the TLC channel's *19 and Counting*. Gary also appears regularly on the program *Prophecy in the News*. Additionally, Gary speaks nationally on various radio programs and was featured in a *Vanity Fair* article. Gary has authored a number of books and video series including *Hell Is for Real, Walking Where Jesus Walked, America at the Tipping Point, It Could Happen Tomorrow, The Divine Appointment, Signs of the Coming of Christ, What Really Happens When Jesus Returns, The Glorious Appearing,* and

The Arab Israeli Conflict. In addition, his *Hell Is for Real* is available as a DVD, and soon his newest books, *The Miracle of Israel* and *The Revelation, God's Final Word* will be released. Gary is also a contributor to the *LaHaye Prophecy Bible* and the *Prophecy Encyclopedia* and along with his friends, Tim LaHaye and Ed Hindson, travels nationally speaking in the "Global Warning Conference on Bible Prophecy" hosted by many of America's largest churches.

On the fun side, Gary is a commercial, multi-engine-rated pilot and an avid golfer.

Gary and his wife, Sandra, reside in Texas and have four children and eight grandchildren.

discoverymissions.org

facebook.com/**drgaryfrazier**

twitter.com/**garyfrazier7**

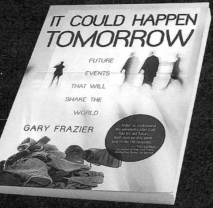